CAPTURED
BY THE
HOLY SPIRIT

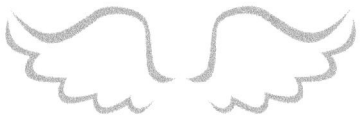

LISA LEIKAM

CAPTURED BY THE HOLY SPIRIT
Copyright © 2015, 2016, 2017 Lisa Leikam
All rights reserved. Except as permitted under the U.S. Copyright Act of 1976, no part of this publication may be reproduced, distributed, or transmitted in any form or by any means, or stored in a database or retrieval system, without prior written permission of the publisher.

ISBN-13: 978-0-692-90366-7
ISBN-10: 0-692-90366-6

TABLE OF CONTENTS

Preface... 9

PART I
SIGNS FOR MY SOUL... 11

Peaceful Easy Feeling
The Sunset Drive
Flowers from Heaven
The Card
Going Home
"333" Angel Number
A Crow
My Guardian Angel
Heavenly Hearts
Is He Looking at Me?
Church
The Chimes
Jesus is My Pilot
"Q" for Questions?
Other Signs and Messages
First of 10
The "First" Rock
A Glowing Lantern
Dogs Go to Heaven Too!
Gone into the Night

PART II
MY SANITY... 31

A New Journey
Lenny's Birthday
A Sun Emoji
Will You Remember Me?
A Crown of Rays
The Last Rites
Time
It Always Works Out
A Military Farewell
"555"
The Birds and the Bolts
What Now?

The Appointment
Believe or Not Believe?
Is This It?
Publishing
A Butterfly Totem Dance
A Gala Invitation
Feathers
The Dominance of Angel Numbers
Forever Hearts
Butterflies and Belief
I Need A Sign
Cry If You Want To

PART III
CAPTURED FOR THE TRUTH... 57

Out of My Control
Moving Forward
My Search
Finding Grace
The Merchandise
Unhappy Vibes
A Sadness I Saw
A Day of Therapy
Seven Sacraments
Week One
Week Two
Dreams
The Figurine and the People
Winfield Festival
So Close to Me
Smoked "Butts"
Soul Mates
A Calling
Progress
Angels
Eternal Life
Miracles
Biography
From the Author
A Special Thank You
This Olé House of Ours 1992
Merry Christmas 2001

TO MY FAMILY...
WITH LOVE

IN LOVING MEMORY OF BROTHER LENNY

It is with great sadness we lost you so soon, and the way you left,
with the unknown of the thereafter.
I write this with comfort that you are at peace
with eternal life in The Heavenly Kingdom
of The Lord Our God.
I love you!

Also in Loving Memory of:

Both of my Dads, Jerome and Clyde,
Brother Ron, Nephew Jamie
And all family members who have gone before us.

PREFACE

I am writing this in March 2015. A few months ago we celebrated another Christmas and I felt blessed with what the Lord has given us and provided us with. The older we get the more we realize how truly blessed we are.

Christmas was different this year. Dad was in the nursing home, my brother Ron passed away a couple of years ago, and my brother Lenny was not present, as is usual for him. For years his hard work in the grocery business kept him away from holiday gatherings. It is their busiest time of year and so it was rare for him to come home for Christmas.

A couple of weeks into January Lenny posted two photos on Facebook. He was feeding ducks at a marsh and included captions with both pictures. His life had been upside down for some time. He had been in and out of jobs since he quit the grocery store he had worked for many years. He had quit that year, in 2007, to make it home for Christmas, surprising us as he loved to do. It was a joyous reunion. After that he never landed a great job again and suffered a difficult divorce. His recent photos on Facebook sent unwanted thoughts through my mind and I wondered what he was thinking.

It all happened so fast: the photos, the random thoughts that Lenny might take his life, and then a sunset, all a sign, now my brother was gone.

As we waited for my brother's body to make it to Kansas I wished on a message on a church sign, saying: "God can do more than you can imagine." Ephesians #3. As I traveled to work, and read that message, I asked God for a sign that my brother Lenny had eternal life.

I received some flowers from Heaven (see later chapter), which was beautiful in so many ways. And that was only the beginning of what was to come. When messages and Angel signs continued to appear it was the beginning of many mystical happenings taking me deep into the depths of the spirit, the soul, and life itself. I had embarked on a mystical journey of receiving messages, signs, numbers, hearts, and the unknown, while experiencing doubt, sanity, and healing for all.

SIGNS
FOR MY SOUL

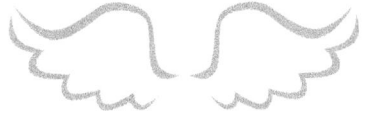

PART ONE

PEACEFUL EASY FEELING

My younger brother Lenny was a fantastic brother, father, son, and friend. He lived in Henderson, Nevada, a suburb of Las Vegas. He left our hometown of La Crosse, Kansas after graduation, never to return to the slower life of the Midwest. He was a grocery store manager for over 25 years. He was 46, divorced, and has a son named Andrew, 21. Lenny was a caring, loving father to Andrew, who was his pride and joy. He loved bowling, golfing, and sporting events. Living in Las Vegas the opportunities were endless, including the one-eyed bandits (slot machines). He was always a character, a joker of sorts, and he loved surprises.

Sadly, distance kept us away from each other over the years. We took great trips to Vegas, and he visited our family here too, but we never experienced the daily, weekly, or monthly visits which the rest of the family is accustomed to. We missed out on so much of his life.

On January 18, 2015 Lenny posted a picture to Facebook captioned, "Peaceful Easy Feeling." He was at a marsh pond somewhere in Las Vegas feeding the ducks. It did look peaceful. And yet something about the picture wasn't right. He looked too serious, which was unlike him, as he always had a fun side. We now realize that through the photos on Facebook, he sent us a message telling us he was leaving, and the "Peaceful Easy Feeling" of where he was going and the peace and eternity he would have there. We later discovered that he had written letters of goodbye while at the pond that day; one for Andrew and one for Mom. He also had his phone set to shut off on January 25.

Several people had tried to call him but he didn't answer his phone. Messages he sent on Facebook were vague. He finally answered my brother's call on January 15, and he later called Mom. He said he was doing okay, but he felt depressed. My brother recalled him not sounding right. He hadn't told anyone until then that he had quit his job in November, believing he had accepted another, only to find out the position was no longer available. As I look back on his Facebook timeline, he told Mom on January 1, 2015 that he loved her very much. I think he knew then that he would take his life. My mind kept telling me to call him, yet I never got around to making the call, and even if I had have called him, I'm not sure if it would have made any difference. The thousands of miles between us, kept us apart. I don't think we were guided to help him as he would soon be free and in the hands of God.

THE SUNSET DRIVE

On Friday, January 23 my husband Al and I headed to Salina to see my family. My Stepdad Clyde was in the nursing home and his health had been steadily declining. He was 89. My Mom remarried a few years after my Dad died in 1977. Clyde brought three children of his own to our family making it a family of ten; five boys and five girls. He accepted us, a family of seven kids, four still at home, and the youngest handicapped. He provided for us, guided us, and loved us. That alone was a true blessing.

My Mom and Dad live on the east side of Salina and it was easiest to take the back way in. We were headed west on Old Hwy 40 and the sun was starting to set. The view was amazing. The clouds were hovering above; there were beautiful colors in the background, and a glowing light at the end of the road. The picture on the cover of *Signs For My Soul* was taken that day. It was pretty, but it also had an eerie look and feel to it.

We reached our turn and we could now see the sunset over the countryside. For some reason, Lenny came to my mind. Someone had recently said he was depressed and struggling, and my mind told me I hoped he wouldn't do anything drastic.

Three and a half days later, on Tuesday, January 27, I received the telephone call to say Lenny had taken his life.

FLOWERS FROM HEAVEN

We had never experienced a loss of someone so far away. Getting a deceased person home from another state is not a fast task. Permits are needed to cross state borders, the flight to Kansas City, and then the trip to our home town of La Crosse, Kansas. Andrew also wanted to have a small goodbye get together in Vegas for family and friends who would not make the trip to Kansas for the funeral. Therefore, we had time to mourn, to cry, to wonder, and ask why. How did this happen? How did we not see it? My brothers, sisters, a niece and a nephew all gathered at Mom's to go through photos. We made a memorial video and reminisced about the good times. We looked back at happier times, the good life he had experienced, and all the wonderful memories he had left behind. He seemed so happy-go-lucky and he was the last person we thought would have committed suicide. The extra time also allowed for us to go home for a few days and get ourselves together. It had already been a long four days and the funeral was still to come.

I hadn't been to work since the initial news of Lenny's death on the evening of Tuesday, January 27, so I hadn't seen my boss or coworker yet. I planned to go in to work on the following Monday, but when I woke up I couldn't find the strength. I hadn't had any time to myself yet and I needed an alone day. I emailed my work and said I would try to go in the next day.

On Tuesday I made it to work and the day went by fast, which was a relief. There is a Christian school and church that we drive by daily. There are always quotes written on it. This week the quote is, "God Can Do More Than You Can Imagine" Ephesians #3. On my way to work on the morning of Wednesday, February 4, as I drove by, I asked the Lord to, "Please give me a sign that Lenny is at peace and in His arms in Heaven." As a Catholic, I was struggling with the unknowns of his suicide. I needed to know, had he gone to Heaven? Was he no longer lost and hurting from the pain he had? Was he at peace with eternal life?

I left work at 5:00 p.m. and stopped by the store to get a few items for supper. I went to the express checkout. After paying I turned around to put my wallet back into my purse as a young gal approached me, her arms extended towards me, holding flowers. She asked if I wanted them. I was in awe looking at the flowers and I took them from her, telling her, "Yes, I most definitely want them." I thanked her and told her she had made my day. I placed the flowers on top of my purse as if they were holy. I turned back to the clerk for my receipt; she had a look of sorrow in her eyes and on her face; and with a sympathetic voice she said, "Have a good day."

When I arrived home I told my husband I had received flowers from Heaven. I cried as I told him the story. He didn't know what to say, do, or think. But as the evening went on, I believe he realized there was no other explanation for the flowers. They were indeed from Heaven.

I cried on and off all evening. Our sons, Chris and Colton, were over for supper. I felt bad, but they understood I was crying for the loss of my brother. However, I don't think they understood the concept of how I had received those flowers. After all, how do you receive flowers from Heaven? That doesn't happen. I placed the flowers in a vase. There were three tulips, two red and one pink, each leaning their own way. They were beautiful.

PART ONE: SIGNS FOR MY SOUL

The next morning, when I woke up, I entered the kitchen to find the three leaning tulips had risen to the sky, two of them hugging in unity, like a brother hugging his sister to comfort her. It was a beautiful sight and so special!

That person who gave me the flowers in the store was a messenger of God. She had no idea what the gesture would mean to me. She most likely did not know that she had been sent to deliver a powerful message from Our Lord that Lenny was at peace and in His arms. It comforted my heart, mind, and soul.

THE CARD

A couple of days after I received the flowers we were outside talking with Colton about arrangements to La Crosse for the funeral. We would meet him and Chris there on Sunday. They were driving together. As we stood there I went to the mailbox and retrieved the mail. There was a card in the

mail addressed to my husband Al. We stood and watched as he opened it, believing it to be a sympathy card, but it was not. We were all surprised to see what it said on the front – Miracles Happen All The Time.

The card was from the Ronald McDonald House®. A card I assume they send out routinely for donations. But today, the timing of it, the message of it, and the circumstances of the last few days with receiving the flowers from Heaven, I believe it was a message to us.

GOING HOME

Lenny's funeral service was on February 9 at 10:00 a.m. It was a sunny beautiful morning for that time of year in Kansas. It was held at the funeral home in La Crosse. Lenny had been away from La Crosse since graduating from high school, so his classmates had moved on and he no longer had any friends who lived there. For that reason, we knew the service would be attended by mostly family and town people.

It was a Catholic service, the same as a church service except there would be no communion. The Funeral Chapel filled up and Mass started with Amazing Grace by Carrie Underwood. Father gave a wonderful lecture on love and kindness. Since we had no organist or singer we used a portable speaker we had purchased at Christmas time. The sound it put out was amazing and we could play the songs we wanted. We also played "Here I am Lord" by Jill Henwood and "How Great Thou Art" by Carrie Underwood. The sound in the cathedral-shaped building echoed off the walls and sent chills down everyone's spines.

Outside, the sun was shining bright; it was about 60 degrees and we couldn't have asked for a more gorgeous day weather-wise. We all gathered in our cars when it was time for the procession to the cemetery, Lenny's final resting place. The priest blessed his body and grave, and prayers were said. We ended with the song Heaven is My Home Now by Libby L. Allen. The song could be heard throughout the cemetery. It was so moving, in the still of the day, and now another brother had gone home.

"333" ANGEL NUMBER

The angel number 333 has been in our family for some time. There are many writings of the number 333 in the Bible. Some say the three threes stand for The Lord Our God, Jesus Christ, and The Holy Spirit, and when you see the numbers you know they are with you, helping you along the path ahead, protecting you and comforting you. That is why they appear more frequently when a loved one has passed.

PART ONE: SIGNS FOR MY SOUL

My sister Kathy lost her son Jamie to a car accident 19 years ago at the age of 18. That was tough and very hard to handle. He was a great kid, and he had so much talent. That is when she began seeing the numbers 333. She would wake to see this number in the middle of the night; she would also see it when she was driving in her car, and on clocks. It literally popped up everywhere. The 333's also appeared when our brother Ron passed, as well as when Lenny passed.

A few days after Lenny's funeral we had taken his son Andrew to the airport for his flight home to Henderson. Mom, my sister Kathy and I made it back to Salina by mid-afternoon and by this time I was ready to head home myself. It had been a long two weeks and we all needed to get back to some form of normality. As I drove down Interstate 70 in silence, thinking, unwinding, and with my mind elsewhere, I reached over to turn the radio on. The clock read 3:33 p.m.

A couple of days later, as I headed home from town, I pulled up behind a box truck stopped at the stop light. I paid no attention until I looked forward to see if the light had turned green. And then I saw on the license plate the number 333.

A CROW

My workplace is a house converted into offices. It is located on a main street with some businesses and residential houses around it. Therefore, there are several mature trees around. One day after Lenny's funeral I arrived at work, parked, and got out to walk to the rear door. In the distance I heard a crow crowing. The next day when I arrived at work, I heard the crow again, but louder than the day before. I looked to see if I could see him, but I could not. On the third day I pulled up again and I heard the crow right away. As I walked down the sidewalk it sounded like he was right above me and definitely wanted my attention. I stopped halfway down and looked up, but still could not see the crow. I smiled towards the direction of the sound, and in a joking way asked, "What are you doing? I obviously know you are there, how could I not?" He did not "talk" back but continued to squawk as I went inside the building. I have not heard the crow since.

This was not the first time I had heard the crow. I experienced the same thing when my brother Ron passed away. At that time I wondered if it was a sign, but never took it much farther. I think that is why the distant sound from the crow caught my ear so fast. Now, I believe it is a sign telling me that my two deceased brothers are very near.

MY GUARDIAN ANGEL

I have become increasingly intrigued with the messages and signs I've been given. I often research signs, angels, spirits, and the passing of loved ones on the internet. I read that you can talk with your Guardian Angel, try to find out its name, and ask it questions. You can ask something in your mind to them and they may give you a sign.

One morning, I was sitting on my bed putting my socks on when I looked up at a picture on my wall of a little girl who reminded me of my sister, Kathy. In my head I asked if my Guardian Angel was called Kathy. I then laughed to myself thinking, *You're losing your mind girl!* As I left the room and headed down the hallway I heard the name of a basketball player being announced on the TV. "Jerome" Jerome? This was my Dad's name and not a name you hear every day. He passed away of a heart attack on November 4, 1977. I was 16 and he was 49. So, is he my Guardian Angel? Was this my sign?

Back in the eighties, when Al and I lived in the Panhandle of Texas, we had only been married a year, and we lived on a ranch in the middle of nowhere. One night I fell ill and had a seizure that made me convulse. Al quickly learned not to put his fingers in my mouth. He said a desperation slap to my face brought me back. It was then that I remembered seeing my Dad. He was a partial figure, dressed in white, like an angel floating in the air. He was offering me a hand, to join him I guess. I did not leave Earth that day, by the grace of God, but maybe, my Dad Jerome really is my Guardian Angel.

PART ONE: SIGNS FOR MY SOUL

HEAVENLY HEARTS

It was Sunday and I was preparing supper. The boys always come over on Sundays for family dinner and on this day I was making Swiss and smothered steak. Using round steak I cut the meat into squares, removed any fat, and breaded for frying. I put the first batch in, cooked it, and removed it from the skillet. I then put the last batch in to fry. I turned to clean the flour up while it cooked and when I returned to the skillet one of the pieces in the center of the skillet was heart shaped. I stared at it, wondering if it was real. I asked Al to come over and asked him what he saw. He replied, "A heart." I did not cut a heart in any way, shape or form. I simply cut the meat, removed the fat, and breaded it. And yet, a perfect heart was right there for us to see, cooking in my skillet!

A couple of days later Al had showered and I had gone in the bathroom afterwards. As I looked down on the tile floor there was a puddle of water in the shape of a heart.

And yet again, as we cooked dinner a few days later; Al cleaning potatoes at the sink while I worked at the island, he turned to get my attention. "Hey Lisa"! I turned to see him holding a potato in the shape of a heart. We both smiled. At this point we knew these were blessings from above to comfort our souls.

IS HE LOOKING AT ME?

Our best friends, Kenny and Cheryl, live in Overland Park, Kansas. We love getting together with them. They are our therapy. We compete as a team with our kids in BBQ competitions, we attend any music venue we can, and we take part in the four-day Bluegrass Festival in Winfield. But mainly, we laugh, be who we are, and enjoy the friendship.

Back in November, Kenny had called Al to see if we would be interested in going to see Bob Seger at the Sprint Center for the "Ride Out" Tour. I had listened to Bob Seger music growing up but could only think of a few songs he played. Either way, we were in. Tickets were going on sale in January and Kenny and Cheryl would get them. As it turned out we ended up in Overland Park the weekend they came on sale and Cheryl and I purchased them together that Saturday at 10:00 a.m.

After Lenny's death, his son Andrew wrote a message on Facebook about how lucky he was to have had a father like Lenny, and that he had turned out just like him.

He also commented, "I hated Bob Seger as a kid, but man I'd be a liar if I told you that Night Moves is not one of my favorite songs." Wow, I didn't realize Lenny was a Bob Seger fan. This made the upcoming Bob Seger concert even more special as it would be in memory of Lenny. On March 18 I posted the event to Facebook with the saying, "This one is for you, Lenny! We will be dancing to Night Moves with Bob Seger and your spirit in the sky! Love and miss you." I'm not sure what I expected. Did I want a sign? Something showing me that Lenny would be there, in spirit? Deep down I know I did, but I also knew the odds.

The concert was Friday, March 20. It was a nice spring day and we took off for Overland Park and Kenny and Cheryl's house around noon. Once we arrived the laughs would begin. We headed towards Power and Light District at around 5:00 p.m. to get something to eat and have a drink prior to the concert. We then headed to the concert at around 7:30 p.m. and found the seats we purchased in section 108, row 12 and seats 1-4. They were awesome seats, off to the side and down low. The concert started at 8:00 p.m. with a pre-lineup band playing first. At around 9:15 p.m. Bob Seger hit the stage and the show began.

I was amazed! I knew every song he was playing, and so did the crowd singing along. The age group appeared to be 45 and older. Even an older grandma sat two rows in front of us dancing to the beat. He totally rocked the crowd!

I used our cell phone cameras to take pictures during the concert. I didn't know what pictures I had taken but thought I might have some pretty good close ups. At one point he was in our corner and had put his hand over his eyes, as if blocking the lights to see into the crowd. I took a few pictures but did not look at them at the time.

We made it home late in the afternoon on Saturday. The NCAA Basketball Tournament had started and we were ready for the comfort of our chairs. As we were sitting there watching the games I looked at the pictures I had taken on our phones. We got a few good shots. As I looked at the last picture it was of Bob Seger, with his hand over his eyes, searching the crowd, and in the picture he appears to be looking directly at me. I couldn't help but think that was my sign; that only through the Holy Spirit could I have taken this picture at the exact right time. Lenny's spirit was at that concert.

CHURCH

Losing a loved one can bring us closer to God as we mourn their loss and ask for comfort and peace. Al and I were raised Catholic, and our sons as well. We come from a family where our grandparent's brothers and sisters were nuns, priests, and a Monseigneur, so religion is a big part of our culture. We attended church in our boy's younger days, but as they grew older baseball tournaments and sports took up our time and we no longer "made" time to attend mass. It's not that we lost our faith; we just got lazy. I believe that because of our continued belief and faith in the Lord, He continues to watch over us, protecting us and loving us unconditionally.

On the Friday after Lenny's funeral Al said maybe we should start going to church again. He didn't have to ask twice. After all we had been through and seen, it was time to thank the Lord for the comfort and peace He had given us. We returned to church that Sunday.

I had read about the changes in Catholic Church Mass but had not yet experienced it. The only masses we had been to recently were either funerals or weddings. So on that Sunday the language was somewhat different, but I liked it. Saying "Spirit" seemed appropriate.

As I prayed on that Saturday night after seeing the Bob Seger picture a voice inside my head told me I needed to share the messages I had been given, to show people what God and the Holy Spirit can do in our presence. On Sunday at church Father's sermon told us to give, share, and spread our talents, hobbies, and love. It was then I absolutely knew I needed to share the experiences we have had.

That day I had plans to work out in the front yard as the bushes needed trimming, the weeds needed to be pulled and cleaned from the winter. I was going to take the portable speaker we used at the funeral to the porch and listen to music while I worked. I turned the speaker on to make sure it was charged. I then went to change my clothes, put my shoes on, and get ready to go. I walked over and picked up the speaker so I could hook it up to the iPad. When I put my hand on the handle to pick it up, it started playing Amazing Grace. I immediately sat it back down.

I hadn't played this song, as I hadn't yet sunk the speaker to Wi-Fi on the iPhone or iPad. There were about 10-15 minutes in between me turning the speaker on and the playing of the song. I brought the speaker further into the living room and turned it up louder, to listen to the song.

THE CHIMES

We live in a cul-de-sac with our house at the very end. The front as well as the garage faces south towards the street. There is a house next to us on both sides, and no houses behind us. The other two houses are further up the road as you enter the cul-de-sac. I spend a lot of time in the garage as I refurbish things and work out of there. I also smoke in there when it is cold out. Therefore, I am accustomed to the sounds of the neighborhood, and in general it is quiet.

Sitting in the garage one day after Lenny's funeral I heard the sound of wind chimes, as if swaying lightly in the breeze directly outside the door. I didn't recall my neighbors having any wind chimes. I sat there and listened. I considered opening the garage door to see where the sound was coming from but I didn't.

The next day, I again heard the chimes playing as I was in the garage. I felt as if I had heard this sound before, in the past. And then it came to me; it was right here, in my garage, when my brother Ron passed.

I have since looked for my neighbor's wind chimes but they do not seem to have any. I have listened with intent, when it is calm, and when the wind blows, but there is no sound of wind chimes.

JESUS IS MY PILOT

I hadn't been to Salina since taking Andrew to Wichita for his flight. Our weekends were either busy or the winter weather had kept us from the trip. I needed to get over to see Clyde. When I arrived he was having a good day. He had been in a nursing home for about a year now, unable to walk and care for himself. Some days his mind was there, and others it was not. We brought McDonalds in for his lunch on Saturday, which he hadn't had in some time. We visited for a while and then I was ready to head home, as I still had weekend chores to complete.

As always, I headed East on Crawford, turned on Shipton Rd, and then headed towards Old Hwy 40, the road we had traveled along many times. There is a railroad track right before you reach Hwy 40. Many times trains switch engines and the track may be tied up for what seems like forever. And this was the case on this particular day. As I pulled up there were cars in line waiting. Some of them were turning around to go back in the direction they came. I pulled up until I was the second car in line and put the car in park; ready to wait as I didn't want to go back. After about five minutes the first car in line started to back up and turn around. She had her window down so I asked how long she had been waiting. She said, "Long enough." I really didn't want to turn around, but I decided it would probably be for the best. I turned around to go back the way I came when I saw the train start to move in my rearview mirror. Now what? Oncoming vehicles were heading towards the tracks and the now moving train. The first vehicle to go by me had a tag on the front of their vehicle that said, "Jesus." With my sense of renewed faith I decided to turn around again and follow Jesus on the roads I knew so well.

I was now right back where I had started. As we waited for the final train car to pass by I looked in my review mirror to see a car pulling up behind me. Dam, it is a Highway Patrolman. I didn't want him following me all the way to Interstate. By now the train had finally cleared the tracks and we were on the move. I pulled up at the stop sign and signaled right, hoping the Highway Patrolman would turn left and head the other way...but he did not!

When he turned right to follow me I asked the Lord to please help me get through this. I knew I had about 15 miles on a two lane highway to go before the turnoff, and if he was going to follow me all the way I would be very uptight. Driving this stretch of highway seemed to take forever. I set my cruise on 57 not knowing what the speed limit was. I clasped the steering wheel tightly with both hands, and drove ahead.

I finally saw the Interstate sign ahead and couldn't wait to get off this road with him right behind me. I turned my right hand blinker on not looking what he was doing. I turned onto the ramp and then I saw him, in the rearview mirror, heading over the bridge in the other direction. I sighed and said to myself, "Thank you Jesus"! Thank you for guiding me through that very trying situation." It took a while for me to calm down but I was finally headed towards home.

I had just passed Junction City and there were merging roads from the City and The Fort. I was driving along in the outside lane with a car in the inside lane barely in front of me. I noticed a car coming down off a merge ramp and wondered what the car next to me would do. He was going to have to move somewhere as the distance between our vehicles was minimal. Since he was not moving over and wouldn't have anywhere to go I stepped on the gas to pass by him. As I did this he came over to get into my lane, his rear end ready to hit my front end. I hit the brake and turned onto the shoulder to avoid being hit. My heart was pounding, my hands were shaking, and I was so ready to be home. I thought to myself it was a good day to follow Jesus. I had no interaction with the Highway Patrolman and I had also avoided a potential accident.

"Q" FOR QUESTIONS

Finally... home sweet home... thank God! It was a long trip but I made it safe and sound. I was catching up with Al on the trip when Colton called. I went outside to talk without the noise of the TV. As I spoke to him I played with the rocks in our landscape with my foot, knocking them back and forth. Suddenly, I saw a rock that caught my eye with the same characters of another rock found recently by my sister. I picked it up, still talking to Colton, but wondering if this too was a sign. We finished our conversation and I went to examine the rock more closely. I wondered if indeed it had a meaning. It looked like a "Q". A "Q" which could stand for question. Maybe Jesus was asking me if I still had questions. After my drive home, following "Jesus," the Highway Patrolman, the near accident, and all the signs he had given me in comfort the last month and a half, did I still have questions? Questions of His power, Lenny's eternal life, and the love and blessings He had given me?

No, I had no further questions. I had no doubt in The Lord Our God. Through the death of His son Jesus Christ we are given guidance and eternal life. Even missing His Sunday services He was still there. He was always there because we never lost our faith to believe in Him and all the good He is, and does. We are so very blessed.

PART ONE: SIGNS FOR MY SOUL

OTHER SIGNS AND MESSAGES

FIRST OF TEN

My older brother Ron passed away on April 30, 2012. He battled heart problems for some time before he was taken home at the age of 57; the first child of ten to pass away. He was a wonderful son, a fabulous dad, a great brother, and an awesome grandpa.

He was a business owner for most of his life. After Dad died he returned home to help run the family business: a bowling alley, a restaurant, and a lounge. Later, he opened his own business in La Crosse called The Whiskey River Club. He also owned Colors by Ron in Wichita, a commercial painting business, until his health no longer allowed him to work. He then helped to raise his grandchildren as if they were his own. He was a very loyal Kansas City Chiefs fan and he had season tickets at one time. He also loved the one-eyed bandits, and football and slot machines were his weekend getaways.

THE "FIRST" ROCK

On March 10, 2015 my sister Kathy text me a picture of a rock she found as she was working in her backyard. It was a flat and smooth rock and had what we both thought looked like a face on it, with sunglasses on, and the look of a photo we had so recently admired. A photo of Ron we used in the memorial video for Lenny's funeral.

THE GLOWING LANTERN

I have a very old, rusty kerosene lantern that hangs in a tree out the back of the house. There is no oil in it, no wick, and is very rusty. It wouldn't work if you wanted it to. On two mornings shortly after Ron's funeral the lantern was glowing, entirely lit up with a bright yellow glow. My mind told me it was the Eternal Light shining upon him.

It seemed the sun was making the lantern glow, although it is hidden back in the trees and I am not sure how the sun was hitting it just right. It was very real at the time, and now, three years later, I realize it was another way of the Lord sending me messages.

DOGS GO TO HEAVEN TOO!

I recently came across another rock when I was doing some yard work. It stuck out when I saw it; the lines in it looked different so I picked it up. After examining it a little further I noticed it had the features of a dog's head. So does this mean after all these years gone by I should know Shakespeare, our pet dog, is in Heaven?

GONE INTO THE NIGHT

Shakespeare was a dog we had for many years. His hair was a wired reddish brown color. He was our first family dog; we got him as a puppy for Chris. He was a good dog. He loved to play fetch, and always wanted attention. Like many dogs, he had a few bad habits, such as darting out of the door, which he was pretty good at. If someone opened the door, he would make a run for it, and resulted in many trips out to try to get him to come home. Sometimes he did, and sometimes we hoped he would make it back on his own.

PART ONE: SIGNS FOR MY SOUL

He was starting to show his age, as he was 14. He had cataracts in his eyes and he could barely see, and his hearing was going too. We talked about the day he would leave us and we all agreed we would have him cremated and put on the mantelpiece. He had been such a great dog and he had been with us for so many years.

One night I let him out the back door to do his duties. I didn't realize the wind had blown open the fence gate and he got out. Chris and I immediately went out into the dark to search for him. We both took our cars to cover a bigger area. He was nowhere to be seen. We searched until there were no more places to look. We woke when the sun came up and started a new search. There was still no sign of him; he had simply disappeared. They say animals go off to die. Was this what he had done? How had he disappeared so fast, now nowhere to be found? After days of looking, and with no success, we realized he had gone.

We didn't get to say goodbye to him or have him cremated like we wanted. After days of crying I put my emotions into a poem.

Gone into the night

So many times you went your way
Out the door, out to prey
Never had you not returned
Something we begun to learn

Your curious nature
Your faith at hand
Never stopping you
Cause you were good

A great companion for many years
Now we cry our lonely tears
No more crowding at our feet
Not even here to save our seat

The pitter-patter on the floor
A sound that won't be heard no more
Now he leads you into the night
On your journey, one last flight

In loving memory of Shakespeare
August 13, 2005

MY SANITY

Part Two

I know what I am seeing.
Other people see what I am seeing.
So why is my mind so questionable?
It's all right here, but it's all so crazy!

A NEW JOURNEY

When a new chapter in life opens un-expectantly you don't know how it will affect you, where it will take you, and what it will bring. You don't know when, where, or how your life legacy will proceed. When Lenny took his life and closed his last chapter here on Earth, a new chapter opened for me. Death and suicide is not new; it happens every day, every second, everywhere. Our family has lost close members beginning at an early age. But this was different, in that it wasn't a natural death. Lenny took his own life and my conscious had warned me beforehand. I was not surprised when I heard the news, but I felt crushed. I asked for one sign of Lenny's eternal peace in the Lord's arms in Heaven. By the end of the day I received flowers. And that was just the beginning of the messages which came my way.

Things didn't stop after the writing of *Signs for my Soul* (Part I). It was printed for my family for Memorial Day, 2015. I had no idea things would continue to happen at such a rapid pace. I began to question my sanity. *Is spirit truly sending me messages? Or am I lost over the loss of my brother?* In my heart I know he is at peace now.

The many signs and messages I received are trying to tell me something; lead me somewhere, but where?

LENNY'S BIRTHDAY

I hadn't spoken with Andrew in a while and I knew his dad's birthday was coming up in two days, so I called him. He said he was "hanging in there." He was going to play a round of golf on Lenny's birthday, to reminisce their good times on the courses. He wanted to get a dog, but hadn't found the right one yet. I shared a few signs with him and he also felt he may be receiving some. I told him I would share them all with him soon, knowing the book was being printed as we spoke, but I wanted that to be a surprise. He said he would send me some pictures from his time playing golf.

The next day I was in the garage when my phone rang. It was a 702 area code number, which is Vegas. I knew it wasn't Andrew as his name would have shown up. I answered the call. A message came on saying, "If you would like to hear a sign of hope please press 1 now." It rattled me; I was shocked at what I was hearing considering the area code and the timing of it. I fumbled with my phone to get the keypad up and the connection was lost. I immediately dialed the number back and got a recording saying, "If you would like to hear our promotion press 1." I hung up!

On May 14, Lenny's 47th birthday, I was off work and had been thinking about him all day. I wished he was here to call so I could hear him speaking on the line. He would probably be telling some phony story, which was typical of him! I was cleaning and next I planned to clean the bathroom and shower. I use SOS pads in the shower as they work great on soap scum. I washed the walls down and placed the SOS pad on the front outside ridge of the tub. I rinsed the walls with cups of water and was ready to clean the bottom. I turned around and reached for the SOS pad; it was lying where I had put it, and it was in the shape of a heart. I stopped. This was nuts; Lenny's birthday, a SOS pad, and a heart – too surreal!

After I had cleaned the bathroom I went to the garage to smoke a cigarette. I sat in my usual chair when my eyes caught sight of something I briefly recall seeing yesterday in the small white trash can next to the furnace. I looked at it closer and it appeared to be a figure on the side etched in by ashes. It had the shape of a body, a figure, with arms extended upwards, the full body below. I took some photos with my phone and had a closer look. I zoomed in on the photos and besides seeing what looked to be a human form, I also saw some strange things within the figure. This was by far the most surreal thing I had seen yet. Later I shared with Al what I had found and seen. I was taken aback by what I had seen and spent the rest of the evening trying to figure out what had appeared in my trashcan and what it meant. Again, today is Lenny's birthday, and the day has not been without surreal happenings.

The next evening Al and I were in the garage talking. The trashcan was still there, I had not moved it. Al decided to blow the leaves off the floor in the garage, which he doesn't do often. I wondered 'Why is he doing that now?' Al was inching closer towards the trash can and I didn't want him to distract it or mess it up. I moved closer to prevent him from blowing air towards that area. When he seemed to be heading directly towards me, and it, I turned and grabbed the trashcan. I could not let him destroy the fascinating thing in there. This seemed to provoke an argument and our evening went downhill from there.

A SUN EMOJI

May arrived fast! Since March I have been on a mission to tell the amazing journey I am on; it's been too incredible not to share.

When I was working on the book, the number sequence 333 was very dominant, as if it was pushing me along. It seems my goal of having the book ready in time for Memorial Day is going to work out and I will be able to mail it to Andrew and take copies to my family. I picked the books up on the Wednesday before.

I returned to my car with the books and put the box on the front seat. I looked to check them out closer. On the cover I noticed something I hadn't seen in the pic-

ture before; an Emoji sun in the sunset, sitting off to the side of the road. I could see the eyes in it. And now with further observation, I realize there is a lot more going on in the photo.

WILL YOU REMEMBER ME?

On May 22 I headed for Salina early in the morning. Mom, Kathy and I were going to La Crosse to decorate the graves, and my aunt was accompanying us. We decorated the graves of my Dad, my grandparents, Ron's, Lenny's, and Jamie's. When we had finished I gave them their books. I had written a personal message in each cover. We talked about the book and the experiences everyone had come across. On the way home I also shared the photos of the figurine in the trashcan. As they observed the pictures it was obvious they could see what I saw. They also saw the many faces in the figurine.

In Kathy's book cover I wrote the book was also in memory of Jamie. His loss started the 333 signs; signs which I believe are from our spirit angels. I returned from Salina late Friday afternoon and stopped by the office to pick up my paycheck. I also stopped at the bank on my way home. As I waited at the drive-thru window a song came on the radio I hadn't heard in sometime. It is my memory song of my nephew Jamie, "Will you remember me?" We played it at his funeral. When my family heard it on the radio driving to La Crosse the morning after his accident, to help plan his service and for his funeral, I knew we needed to play it; the song now had a meaning. So as I sat there and listened, I couldn't help but tell myself it was a thank you from Jamie for remembering him.

A CROWN OF RAYS

We were headed to Salina again to see Clyde and family as Clyde was not doing well. When we arrived we saw his frail and lifeless body lying in the bed. It was apparent his time to depart this world was near. We stayed for the day but had plans on Saturday and needed to return home that night. I planned to return on Sunday. Prior to leaving Al told Mom she needed to have the priest come to give him the last rites. It was obvious he would soon be passing on. In the Catholic religion the soul is anointed before dying to remove all sins, and to ensure the person dies with Christ and eternal life; something Lenny had not received.

Later that night, when we were home, Chris, who was spending the weekend at Milford Lake, sent me a picture of a sunset. It was a crown of rays shining behind the clouds. I texted him back and told him it was a sign of where Clyde was going and the beauty he would see there.

THE LAST RITES

I returned to Salina on Sunday at around noon. It looked like Clyde would pass on at any time. Mom tried to call the church on Saturday to have the priest come but because it was the weekend he did not answer. I then made a few calls myself with no success. My brother Gary and I decided we would go to Mom's church to see if anyone might be there. There was not. We decided to head to the cathedral also, just in case.

As we drove past the cathedral we saw people in the front of the church foyer so we parked and went inside. It was apparent a baptism or first communion may have gone on. We walked around to see if we could find another priest without bothering the one communicating with the family there. Unable to see anyone we returned to the foyer and waited to the side, admiring the beauty of the old church. Father noticed us and walked our way. I recognized him. He was young, tall, had a beard, and a nice big smile; I had seen his picture in the Catholic Register a couple of weeks earlier. The article had said he was to be ordained into ministry.

As he approached us I told him I recognized him from the paper. He told us he had been ordained yesterday, had given his first mass that morning, and had now baptized his niece. That gave me goose bumps! We congratulated him on his wonderful accomplishments. We explained our situation, needing to have the last rites done for our dad. He called Mom's parish priest but was unable to reach him. He asked where he needed to go and that he would be there as soon as he had finished there. We thanked him and returned to the nursing home. On our drive back to the nursing home I told Gary that if the picture of Chris' sunset had any significance in the days until Clyde's passing, he would die on Monday.

Father arrived fast; he must have left immediately after us. We introduced the family and we all said The Lord's Prayer; Father gave the last rites by anointing his forehead and blessing him. Clyde was 89 and the value of his life became a struggle. As much as we didn't want to lose him we knew he couldn't stick around forever.

It was a day Father will forever cherish and remember. He gave his life and faith to share in his first mass; he brought his niece into Christ with performing his first baptism; and he anointed Dad with the end of life. I can only think he was put there for us, and us for him. The Lord puts people where they need to be, when they need to be there.

TIME

In light of how things looked, I called my boss to let him know I would be staying the night with Mom at the nursing home. We were up until we could no longer keep our eyes open; it was 4:00 a.m. He was resting comfortably and the aides were in and out all night. She took the recliner and I climbed on top of the other bed in the room; his roommate had been moved. It was a short night and he held his own.

Time was passing and the day was getting later. Clyde was hanging on. By 3:00 p.m. I decided to head home to work the next day as it is apparent we would be having a funeral. I said my goodbyes to Clyde, and family, and left, returning home at around 4:30 p.m. I called in to work before they closed to let them know I would be in tomorrow morning.

PART TWO: MY SANITY

I was in dire need of a shower by now, having slept in a nursing home all night. I was unpacking my bag and preparing to shower when my phone rang. It was Mom and she was crying; Clyde had passed away at 5:00 p.m., on Monday, June 1.

Everyone had left, leaving Mom and the aides with him. The aides were off duty but came in to see him as they knew his time was near. They liked him and were good with him. Clyde waited until all the kids left as he didn't want to die in front of us.

IT ALWAYS WORKS OUT

Sometimes things seem to work out the way they are supposed to. We had the week of June 1 on our calendars for five years as Al's hometown holds an Old Settlers Reunion every five years for school classes to hold reunions. It's great getting together with everyone you don't live close to, but still keep in contact with.

With Clyde dying on Monday, Mom wanted to go to La Crosse on Wednesday to make arrangements for the funeral. This worked out for us. Al and I planned to meet them at the funeral home. Chris would leave behind us so he could pick Al up in La Crosse and head to Ness City from there. I would stay and drive over when we were done and we could still attend the festivities.

After making arrangements at the funeral home we went to the cemetery and City Hall for the lot, then to the flower shop to order flowers. We will use our speaker for the service music and I downloaded some songs for them to hear. We listened to them as we drove around; they brought tears to our eyes but mother liked them. We finished everything and then headed our separate ways. They headed back to Salina and I headed to Ness. We planned on meeting back there on Friday afternoon to prepare for the nightly vigil.

This worked out the way it was supposed to. Mother wanted simple, unlike what we did for our brothers where we had video's, pictures, and lots of personal music. Mom and I had engaged in some discussions prior to Clyde dying, which had caused some tension. We were fine, but since I tend to take the lead, and she wanted simple, and there wasn't much left to do, it worked out fine.

A MILITARY FAREWELL

Clyde was a veteran in the Marine Corps serving in World War II. He was awarded a Purple Heart after suffering injuries in battle at Okinawa, Japan. He was a war hero! We planned for a military service at the cemetery.

The funeral service was at 11:00 a.m. on Saturday, June 6 at the Funeral Home Chapel. The weather was a typical June day in Western Kansas; warm with a hot breeze. Mass was held by the same priest who did Lenny's funeral. Service started with the playing of "Make Me a Channel of Your Peace." Once again Father gave a great sermon. We had visited with him on Wednesday and reminisced stories of Clyde and the family.

And here we were again, driving down the same funeral procession road in La Crosse that goes from the funeral home to the cemetery. When we arrived three Marines were waiting for us. Two marines folded the flag and said goodbye to their comrade, while the third marine was in the background and played taps, an army song played at all military funerals by a member of the military. It gave me, and others, goosebumps. We ended with the song "Go Rest High on the Mountain" as the Marines marched in unison down the road, and out of sight.

"555"

I've been noticing more and more angel numbers recently, but the boldest number sequence is 555. It appears frequently on license plates, clocks, cell phones, and receipts. On the way home from work today I saw a 555 license plate. I pulled up behind a car at the stop light and waited to turn off the highway towards home. As I sat there I thought about the numbers I'd seen that day and wondered if they were real. In my mind I said, if these numbers are truly angel numbers, show me another one on the next vehicle that passes on my right; a white Ford pickup with a license plate of 111 went by!

◆ ◆ ◆ ◆ ◆

It's June 11 and again I headed to Salina. As I was on I-70 just past Junction City I came upon an older car. As I neared it I noticed the license plate number was 555. I signaled to go around and as I was passing a song on the radio caught my ear, "Peaceful Easy Feeling," Lenny's message song. I immediately reached for the radio to turn it up. The time was 3:33 p.m. I was somewhat shaken at all of this happening all at once. I told my family about it when I got there, calling it the "mother-load" of signs. My brother Gary asked what the fives stood for, and I said "change." The number sequences mean change is coming.

THE BIRDS AND THE BOLTS

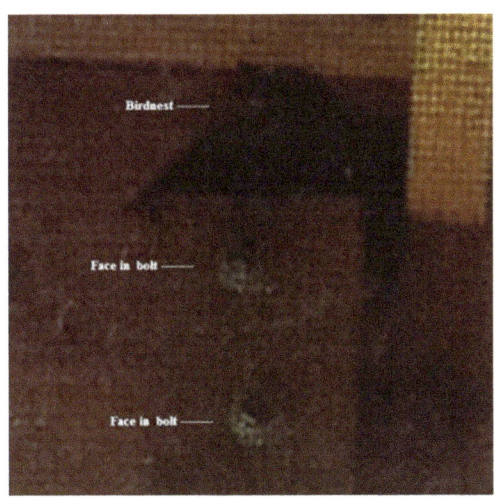

It has been a couple of years since the birds built a bird nest in between the wooden posts of our overhead cover outback. They return each year. Tonight I was out back and heard babies chirping from inside the nest. I took my phone and reached up high to get a picture. When I enlarged the picture I noticed the center of the bolts in the wood rather than the baby birds in the nest.

WHAT NOW?

Everything was starting to wear on my mind. Why did I keep seeing these signs and what were they telling me? I reached out to the religious community by email looking for answers about the spirit world, but received no responses.

What should I do, where should I go? Who will truly understand all this? Maybe I needed to contact someone who dealt with and understands the spiritual world, such as a psychic or medium.

THE APPOINTMENT

I decided to find a psychic/medium. I found one online and called the number, explaining what had been going on since my brother's suicide. I booked an appointment to see the psychic the next day.

The next day I felt nervous. I didn't want to know anything bad, such as when I am going to die; I just wanted to know the meaning behind everything that had been happening. I chose the palm reading and brought my book plus my iPad where all my photos are stored.

The psychic observed the photos. She asked if I recognized the people, and I replied no. She asked if I believed in reincarnation. I shrugged and stated I hadn't thought about it. She then placed her hand on my book and said it was special.

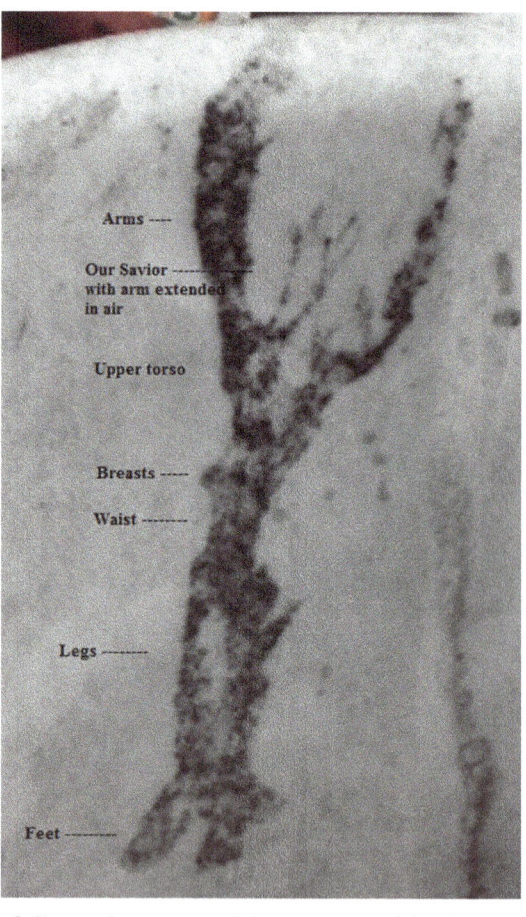

We began with me stating my full maiden name. Then I was told of many things of my past which were true, and also some things destined to occur in the future. She said change was coming, but first something needed to happen. She picked up my book, *Signs for my Soul*, and flicked through the pages. She said it was special and that it would be published and bring monetary value to me. Apparently, the book would help many people.

As I left my mind was racing. So much had been said that was true, yet there were still so many unknowns. How would it play out? I should have asked more but I was in a daze. There was also a concern in regard to one of our sons, which I didn't want to hear.

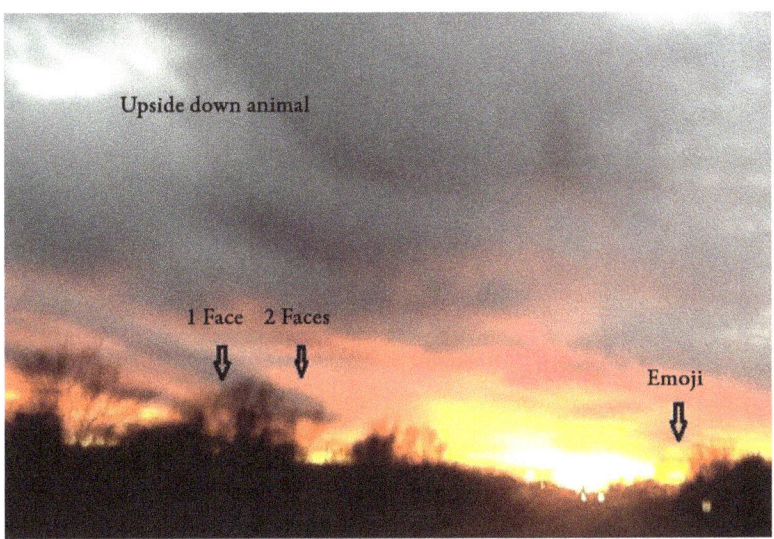

BELIEVE OR NOT BELIEVE?

After the appointment I searched on the internet, "How to tell if a psychic is real?" It told me that a true psychic will "tell" you about the events in your life, whereas a fake psychic will "ask" you questions and then tell you the things you want to hear.

My visit began with me listening about my childhood and my past, and I received some answers as to why these things were happening. I hadn't said a word. Therefore, I decided to believe what was said.

IS THIS IT?

The Lenexa BBQ cook off had arrived again, running on June 26th and June 27th. This is the cook off we do every year with our friends Kenny and Cheryl and the kids. This year our chicken, cooked by their son Chance, took fourth place! There were 183 teams entered so getting your name called and to go on stage, that is a thrill! This was the highest ranking yet after 18 years of entering (ten for our family).

As we drove out of the parking lot on Saturday to head back to Manhattan my phone rang. It was Colton who did not attend this year. He wondered if we were back in town yet. I explained we were just leaving. He said he and his friend Jordy were in a car wreck close to our house and they needed to be towed. My first reaction was, "Are you okay?" They were shaken up but fine. They didn't have their seatbelts on, and Jordy, who was driving, flew across the seat and hit the passenger side of the windshield with his head, shattering it. He was okay, but bleeding slightly. This also meant he landed in Colton's lap. Thankfully they were both okay, just a little banged up.

The right front steering ball joint went out on his truck, which made him lose control of the short bed. They had been on a dirt road cruising to Pottawatomie County Lake just before. The vehicle lost control in the dirt and ended up down a steep embankment. They managed to pull it out before we returned to town, but the truck was a total loss. The first thing which came to mind was, *Is this what the psychic saw and had concerns about?* Now maybe my mind could let go of the "what may be coming?"

PUBLISHING

It seems that publishing a book is a difficult process. After what the psychic said I signed up to a website where companies match your story to publishing companies. Before long, my phone began ringing with companies wanting me to buy their publishing packages. This seemed like an expensive adventure.

Now that I was on the emails list I started receiving emails about how to publish a book through an agent. The first step was to write a query letter, and proposal to agents, pitching why they should read your book, and help to find a publisher for it.

There are lists of agents who represent certain genres (fiction, non-fiction, romance, sci-fi, self-help, and so on) and you need to search those who work with your genre and then submit your manuscript for consideration. I started compiling a query and proposal letter.

I had been working diligently all week on a great query and proposal. I read that agents receive millions of submissions a year, yet unless you're an established author, or a name in the industry, your story usually goes to the delete file. Oh well,

I had never been afraid of trying. On July 14 I emailed out four query letters and proposals, but I ran out of time that evening to send more.

The next day, I continued searching the internet for articles on publishing and I came across an article on self-publishing verses agent publishing. It seemed I might be better off self-publishing as that would result in more money in my pocket in the long term.

My cell phone was still ringing with self-publishing companies. I hadn't been answering them lately but today I was home and a call came in so I answered. I listened to the offer and told him I wouldn't be ready for a couple of months.

A BUTTERFLY TOTEM DANCE

The cotton trees in Kansas were blowing cotton around, which was collecting on everything, including the screens of our back porch. It was a nice day weather-wise; cool for July in Kansas, so I decided to attempt to vacuum the screens, which I hadn't done in the four years since we had screened in the porch. I grabbed the vacuum cleaner and our famous speaker for music and headed out back. After I started, it appeared they would clean up nicely except I couldn't reach the top of the screen. I needed the step ladder and retrieved it from the house. I climbed to the top to begin and saw speckles on the wood above the screen; they looked to be in the shape of a heart! I began cleaning the screens.

I finished the top part of the screen and stepped down, leaving the vacuum on, and then I moved the stool to the next panel. As I looked down to move the vacuum cleaner I saw a butterfly next to me on the walkway. I watched it for some time before turning the vacuum off. I adjusted the stool to sit down watching the butterfly that seemed to be dancing to the song on the radio. When the song was over, the butterfly stayed. I told it I was going in to get my phone if it wanted to stay. I hopped

up, run inside, grabbed my phone, and returned outside. The butterfly was still here. I adjusted the stool to my liking and it jumped, moving over to the grass. Darn! But I was still going to record and see what happened.

I started video recording the butterfly on the grass not far from the walkway. Within a few seconds he came back to the walkway, again looking like he wanted to dance to the music. The song "A Simple Man" by Lynyrd Skynyrd started playing on the radio. He moved a little and then jumped forward, and again moved, like he knew I was recording and he wanted to be in view. I was crying by the end!

It was amazing the way he moved to the music and the beat. I couldn't control my emotions. I run inside bawling and Al thought something was wrong. I told him he needed to come out and see the dancing butterfly. Through the screen he saw the butterfly moving to the music and agreed that it was a dancing butterfly. The butterfly then appeared to clap his wings to Al's answer. "Look at that," I said, "he's clapping to your answer." We both laughed. We watched for a while longer then I continued out of the screen door to record with my camera. Al stayed and watched before returning inside a few minutes later. I didn't record for long with the camera. I had the video I needed and was engulfed in what was happening; to me it was truly beautiful.

The video was the second of three songs danced to that day and was recording at 5:55 p.m. It is available for viewing on YouTube under Amazing Spirit Butterfly Totem Dance.

https://youtu.be/PW1Z6BsOxuc

A GALA INVITATION

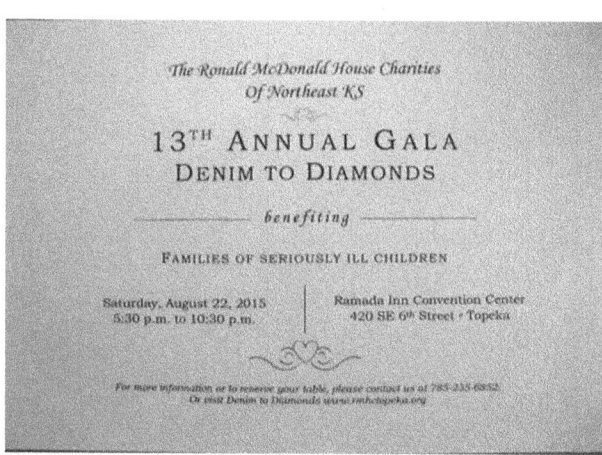

I shared the Ronald McDonald House® "Miracles Happen" card we received at such a timely time with the flowers, and today, July 27, we received another one. Never before have we been on their mailing list. This time it was an invitation to the

13th Annual Gala "Denim to Diamonds" Benefit to be held on August 22 in Topeka, Kansas. Notice the "22." I studied the card and the theme of the event, wondering what it could be telling me.

We went to Chicago this summer and when walking the many streets to get to the L-train on our way to the Cubs game we passed a Ronald McDonald House®. When I saw the name on the building it came to me. My brother's name is Ronald. Could it be his spirit sending me messages via a card with his name on it? When he passed I had first began noticing the signs; the lantern, the crow, and the chimes, so maybe he was sending me messages with the cards.

FEATHERS

Feathers can also be a message from your spirit angels telling you they are near, offering their support and guidance. There is a floor fan in our bedroom on Al's side of the bed and I turn it off every morning. One morning I walked to his side of the bed to turn it off, and lying directly in my path was a rather large white feather, halfway between me and the fan. I picked it up wondering if this was my newest sign.

I went to Salina the next day, returning the following day. Upon my return I went to the bedroom bathroom where there was another white feather lying exactly where it would be seen. But then I remembered we had recently purchased a new mattress pad for our bed and so I began to wonder whether the feathers came from that. I thought so. My mind said, "If they're truly angel feathers I need to find another one outside of the house."

An hour later I went to the sunroom out back to have a cigarette. I usually sit in the rocker, but on this day I went to the couch instead. As I sat there and smoked my cigarette, I looked down towards the floor and noticed something sticking out of the couch on the rope trim. I reached down and pulled it out; yes, it was a very small feather.

THE DOMINANCE OF ANGEL NUMBERS

I was in the process of changing my twitter account photo and biography when I noticed I had posted a tweet about the book coming soon, on July 13th, at 11:11 a.m.

◆ ◆ ◆ ◆ ◆

When I went to Chicago with Al for an association conference he is a member of, from the time we left the house to the time we got back, we saw so many angel numbers…and hearts too!

We made it to the Manhattan airport for our flight and Al pulled into a lot to find a place to park; he saw a space ahead and headed for it. As we got closer we can notice the car next to the parking spot had the license plate 222.

◆ ◆ ◆ ◆ ◆

Smoking is hard to do today in public places, which is good, but it can be a pain if you are a smoker. On our first morning I made my tea, got ready, and headed to the smoking area in front of the hotel. It was off away from the front doors, close to where the valet cars are parked until they are moved further. The car parked there this morning had the tag 444.

◆◆◆◆◆

I was waiting on the spouse of Al's co-worker to tour the downtown area while the guys were in sessions. Once she arrived, we walked to the Magnificent Mile, which consists of retail shops, eating places, and offices; most of the shops were out of my league, even on the sale rack, but it was fun looking around. We walked, we talked, and we saw the sights. Over lunch I brought up the powerful events which had been occurring in my life. She had also lost siblings at a young age and questioned the whys. We saw a building for sale named 444 and I had to get my picture; we saw hearts in the sidewalks and on buildings, and we saw lots of numbers. Even her receipt from Walgreens had been printed at 1:11 p.m.

◆◆◆◆◆

When we were in Salina a few weeks ago the family went out for dinner; the tables were numbered and ours was number 22. The next day we went for lunch and our order number was 22; and at our table was an advertisement for an event which was being held on the 22nd. Three sets of 22 in a short period of time. My mom was shaking her head chuckling; my brother Gary said, "You got it going girl;" and my sister Kathy didn't say much.

Angel numbers have many meanings; each with various messages about what is going on in your life, how you may deal with certain situations, where you may be headed, or what may be within your reach. They can come in many ways with the triple digits the most common; double digits, series, times of day, and any number you see three times within a short period of time; three being "third time's a charm," hence the 333.

I have read up on all of the number sequences, as I had to. I kept seeing so many of them everywhere that I needed to understand what they were telling me. Change is definitely coming!

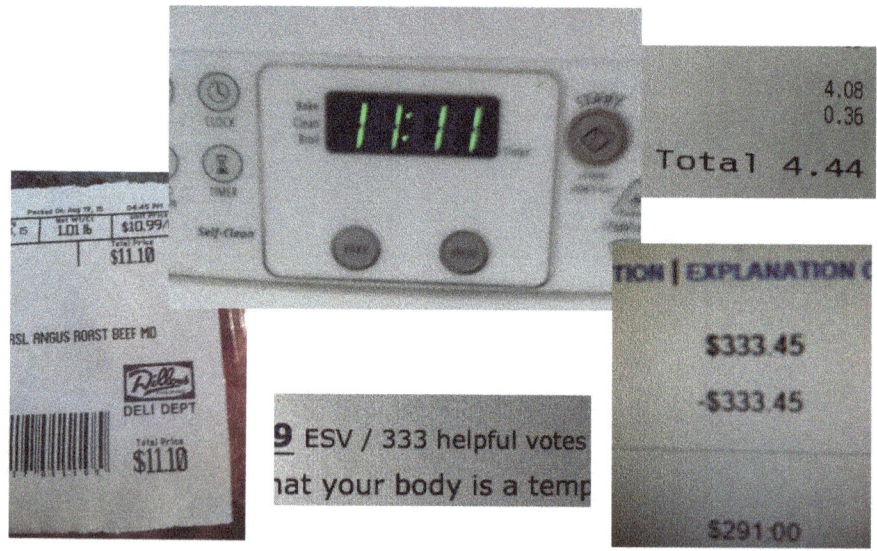

PART TWO: MY SANITY

FOREVER HEARTS

Earlier I shared some hearts, yet there are many more. We planted an area of new grass in the front and backyard after adding dirt for some low spots. As I was preparing to water one day, I saw an area where there was no grass. I walked over and saw a heart-shaped area that hadn't been filled in.

◆ ◆ ◆ ◆ ◆

We went to Colorado for the 4th of July weekend with some good friends from back home. We heard the fireworks were good and they were awesome. A couple of times the smoke rings made hearts, and then a double heart.

I took a photo from outside our hotel showing the river walk with the clouds in the background. I hadn't looked at the picture closely until I saved it on the computer. It was then I saw the heart in the clouds.

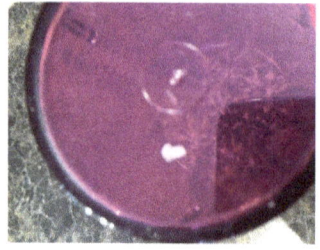
I purchased some drinking glasses with the tags stuck on the bottom; I pulled the sticky tag off one and what remained was a small piece of paper, in the shape of a heart.

◆◆◆◆◆

We were leaving for the Manhattan airport. We were in the running vehicle when I realized I needed to make a last minute trip to my car to close the garage door. Al gave his remote to Chris for easy access. I headed for the driver's side of the car, and there, in front of my car door, was a small heart made of dirt or mud, sitting so I could not miss it without stepping on it. It was perched up with a piece of straw.

◆◆◆◆◆

We returned from Chicago and I went out back to make sure everything was intact and to have a cigarette. I opened the screen door and a small rock was lying in the dirt right outside the door. I could not miss it as it was heart-shaped.

BUTTERFLIES AND BELIEF

Within two weeks of putting mother's house on the market, it sold. She had rented a carefree condo, which was a relief. We headed over to help her get rid of the

PART TWO: MY SANITY

things she would not be taking to her new place. My sister Sherri and her daughter were also coming from Wichita to take some things.

The guys were playing golf in the morning so while they golfed we rented an appliance dolly to haul an old refrigerator out of the basement, which had been there since they moved in. It was old, large, and heavy. One stair at a time they bounced the heaving thing up. Once they made it to the top they all caught their breath than continued through the house and out the garage door.

Mom, Kathy, and I followed a few minutes later. I opened the garage door for Kathy and me to go out, and there, directly outside the door something was lying. I yelped and backed up, unsure what it was. We looked closer and saw it was a butterfly with something on it. We soon realized it was a fake butterfly with lint on it. It had been a magnet at one time, as I remembered when it had hung on the refrigerator. At this same time Kathy said, "Look, a dragonfly" as it flew in, and then out of the garage.

They bounced that heavy refrigerator step by step up the many stairs but the butterfly didn't fall out. They pulled it across the house, but it didn't fall out there. It didn't fall out after bouncing down the first concrete step going out to the garage, or the second. It fell out after all of that, farther out in the garage directly in front of the door for the next person out to see, which happened to be me.

◆ ◆ ◆ ◆ ◆

Papers and documents accumulating by the boxful needed to be shredded, or burned. It seemed it would be easier to burn then haul them away. When I got home tonight Al had started a fire in the fire pit out back. Once it was hot enough we started throwing handfuls of papers and envelopes in. In the stack of papers was one of my original transcripts of *Signs for my Soul*. I had kept almost everything from the writing of it, but there were so many edited copies, there was no need to keep them all. I placed the manuscript on one of the planks, laying it out flat. I watched it burn from the four corners in as I thought of everything that has happened since I wrote it. Now there was so much more to share. As I looked up and away I noticed something on my shoulder. It was a beautiful, large butterfly. This was no ordinary butterfly.

The butterfly totem is said to be the symbol of the soul. It can mean personal change. It can help us to look at things from a different perspective knowing that new and wonderful things are in view. And it is a sign for you to have faith.

While the amazing Butterfly Totem Dance meaning was emotional with feelings at the time, it is now through guidance I understand the freedom that came with it.

I NEED A SIGN

I had still not received an email reply from an agent regarding my book, so I had given up on that. I now believe that was only the beginning of the story as so much more had happened since that I either had to add to the book, or write a sequel. While I was in the bathroom getting ready for work this morning, I asked for a sign again; how will my book publish?

Work was semi-busy. The printer and fax machine are in the front office which is where I retrieve documents and faxes. I was there retrieving papers at around 10:30 a.m. when I returned to my desk and noticed my cell phone showed a missed call. Someone had left a voicemail. I listened to the message and it was the gentlemen from the self-publishing company I spoke to back in July. He wanted to know how my book was coming along. So it seemed I would be self-publishing!

CRY IF YOU WANT TO

Al had never been to Chicago in his life. But we went two weeks ago for his conference and now he was headed back there again. He left early this morning and it had been sometime since I was home alone. I wasn't afraid of staying alone, but the evenings would be long.

When I got home from work, the house was quiet. I didn't have anything to do or anywhere to go and I felt sorry for myself. Before long tears were filling my eyes.

PART TWO: MY SANITY

I tried to deter the sadness I felt and I looked in the fridge to see what to prepare for supper; there was absolutely nothing in it, not even butter for toast and eggs. I needed to regroup and go to the store.

I headed to town with a long grocery list. Once inside the store, I got my cart and headed for the aisles. The first aisle I come to was the deodorant aisle. The Hallmark cards were on the opposite side. As I turned into the aisle my eyes immediately went to the card side where one card caught my eye. It read, "If you wanna cry, fine." Wow, how appropriate as that's what I had been doing about 20 minutes ago. I continued down the aisle and got my deodorant. I turned around and went back to see what the rest of the card said.

The front top part had a girl with a tissue wiping her eyes with the saying above. The bottom part said, "If you wanna scream, fine." I opened the card and it said, "If you wanna do tequila shots and accidentally end up in Vegas with me, super-crazy fine!" Oh how I wish I was in Vegas with my brother (if only he were still here), to do a shot of tequila. I wanted to start crying again, but I don't. Lenny had given me permission to scream too, but I held my composure, put the card in my cart, and moved on.

I had got all the groceries on the list and went to check out. My bill was $85.55. I headed for my car to load the groceries in the back. I lifted the hatchback and moved to pull my cart closer. On the asphalt I noticed a spot of oil, or something, which looked like a heart. I unloaded the cart, got into my car, and sat there for a while, trying to comprehend what had just happened. How did "that" card say what it did; why was I drawn to it; and how much crazier can it get?

CAPTURED FOR THE TRUTH

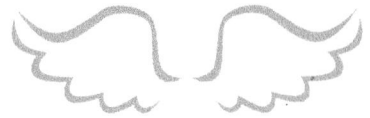

PART THREE

The truth is ...

OUT OF MY CONTROL

After Al's second trip to Chicago, the boys were here for supper. We were catching up as dinner finished cooking. I brought out the card I felt I was led to at the grocery store this week. As he is a busy teenager and college student, Colton had not read *Signs for my Soul*. Therefore, he didn't know what had been going on, other than the few things I had spoken about when they had been over. His first response after I told them the story, and read the card to them was, "Mom, you're thinking way too much."

My boys didn't know I was no longer in control. My every movement, every thought, every notion was engulfed in the photos, the presence of numbers, hearts, events, and the spirit that drives them. It was out of my control; my mind had been taken hostage. As I told Al one day, I wasn't seeking it out; it appeared in front of me. I couldn't run away from these signs; they had captured me. Spirit had taken control and was leading me on my journey.

MOVING FORWARD

Next week is September and I know no more than I did back in June as far as publishing my book, or the people and the faces. In order to move forward I needed to talk to the psychic, so I went for another palm reading. Before we started, I told her that much more had happened since our last visit but I did not elaborate. I said I needed to continue the book, and include some of our visit.

Questions from the last reading were asked and then some things were said, which I didn't understand. I responded with, "What did you say?" She repeated the words as a chart was shown to me: "You have blocked chakras." What the heck is a chakra?

In order to get where I needed to be my blocked chakras needed to be opened; apparently three were blocked. This is not what I was expecting. I was told the treatment could be started immediately.

We spent time talking about the treatment and why it needed to be done. If I left my chakras blocked, nothing would change. I wasn't quite sure I wanted change, as I had a good life. I had a great husband, terrific boys, faith in God, and my health. Besides, what needed changed? I explained I couldn't do anything tonight. I thought if I went home and told Al I had spent money for chakra opening treatments that would probably be the end of it, and me.

When I returned home Al was curious about the outcome. He asked, "How about that book?"

I said, "Yes Al, it's going to be published." I told him I was told I needed therapy along with the cost. He shrugged his shoulders in indifference. But I did not tell him what type of therapy was suggested – opening my chakras.

MY SEARCH

The internet is my favorite place to go to find answers. That night I took to the internet to search for what a chakra was. How that could affect me, and how and why I was supposed to change? The first place I discovered was The Tree of Life, which took me back to my younger days of religion classes, church, rosaries, praying, living the way of the Lord, The Ten Commandments, confession, church, and our religion; to believe in God and what He represents.

The next thing I came across was the chakra chart I had been shown, which depicted the seven chakras, each affecting certain parts of the body. It showed the location of each chakra, the problems they can cause, and the emotions and illness that can occur as a result. As I read through each category I found myself and my health in numerous categories. Is this all true, I wondered?

The next website I went to described the chakras; the energy of life; the batteries to your body; and the power of life. It talked about the sun being your charger, how deep the soul goes, and the need to release any negative emotions you hold as otherwise they could affect your everyday living and your health. It said if you can change your energy you can change your health, your life, and your happiness.

I now realized the change was with me. The something needing to happen first was within me. But I had thought the change would be the rewards of publishing my book; to sell it, bringing in money. Everyone's dream right? But it looked like something in me needed to change, and I knew I was being led the way.

PART THREE: CAPTURED FOR THE TRUTH

FINDING GRACE

I'd read enough information, taken notes, and watched some videos, and I was going to try a few things to see if they would help. I wrote down some self-help affirmations to repeat in order for the three chakras to be unblocked. I wrote down the names of some crystals I needed, and certain incense.

Al and I hadn't yet talked in depth about my appointment two nights ago. As we sat out back this evening I brought it up. I also explained about the chakra information I had found on my internet search. He had thought I was sad and depressed. Well, I guess I did say I needed therapy. He didn't understand how I could be so unhappy. I stopped him, saying I wasn't unhappy at all. I had the best husband ever, I couldn't be prouder of our boys, and I had a wonderful life and home. What more could I ask for?

He was clearly mistaken regarding my feelings. I told him how amazed I was, and how blessed I felt that everything was leading me somewhere. How many people get the opportunity to be led by the Holy Spirit, through God, with messages and signs on their way to finding grace?

THE MERCHANDISE

I don't work Fridays so I went to a shop in town to buy the crystals and incense. When I arrived, I realized I had left my list at home detailing the names of the crystals and incense. I looked at the product selection in the shop and recognized a few names, so I bought some hoping they were the correct ones.

There was an entire wall of incense. I worked my way down the wall to look for a chakra sign, and finally at the end of the wall I found lots of chakra incense. I bought two packages. I also saw a bracelet with colored beads on it and a silver moon star. I grabbed that too, paid, and left.

When I get home I found a small felt bag with strings and put the stones inside. I put the bag in my pocket, the bracelet on my ankle, and that night I took a bath with incense burning. During my internet searches it was interesting to find that most Bishop's and Cardinal's have chakra stones in their Episcopal rings. Another interesting find is that the twelve foundation stones of the New Jerusalem Wall are made of many precious stones and they carry many spiritual meanings, which tell me there could be a spiritual connection.

UNHAPPY VIBES

Mother finally closed on her house at the end of August. It was a late afternoon closing so we did not go that day as she was unsure when she would be able to start moving into her new place. I told her and Kathy to let us know once they knew and then we would head over. Colton was playing in a softball tournament in the morning and if she couldn't get into her new place yet we would go to his game and then leave from there.

The game was at 8:00 a.m. in the morning. We hadn't heard anything from my mother or Kathy so softball it was. Actually I ended up opting out of going to the game, as it was early and I still needed to pack a bag. We would come home the next day. Al and I had talked the night before about stopping in Junction City for breakfast on our way over. Since we hadn't heard from them by the time we left we stopped to eat.

After we ordered, I got my phone out and noticed I had a text from my brother Gary at 10:30 a.m. saying, "Well we are all moved." I text him back saying, "Wonderful, we love showing up when it's done." (There is a family joke about us showing up late to help unload Kathy and Doug when they moved to Salina; by the time we got there they were done.) We ate quickly and got on the road.

When we arrived it was close to lunchtime and they were eating. They all seemed somber. We checked out her new place as they ate. We went downstairs and Al and I spoke about the strange vibes we both felt.

We decided to go get a load from the house. We made a couple more trips before Sherri and Briana arrived from Wichita as they had come to help also. After a few more trips we took a break on Mom's new patio. We got off on another conversation and tension arose.

PART THREE: CAPTURED FOR THE TRUTH

It had been a long month with so much to do; showings, the sale, inspections, paperwork, and the packing. Our summer had been full. Thank goodness Kathy and Doug lived there. They had been her saviors and had the time to help her, to make sure everything was repaired and ready to sell, and to guide her through the process.

We took the last load of furniture over. She had movers coming Monday to move the larger items. Sherri and I sat on the back porch and talked. She wanted to hear of my newest happenings. I began telling her of the recent events; the newest visit, the chakras, and what they represent. I told her the name of the book I was led to, and was reading. I showed her the stones I had in my pocket. She was happy for me, yet she was also sad, and she started crying. She felt unhappy with her own stamina, her self-esteem, and desired to change in the way she felt. I told her she needed to read the same book I was reading. I found it in my searches on the chakras and I had just begun to read it.

We all went to Salina with the intention of staying until Sunday. But we decided to head home later, once everything was done. We relayed our decision and Sherri also decided to head home. There was not much more to do and it was evident everyone was tired. Besides, mother wanted to put things away herself now. When we got home I took a bath to relax and release the day.

A SADNESS I SAW

Something was happening. My mind and body were energized yet I felt so relaxed; I thought about how our trip to Salina went and how sad everyone appeared, each with their own problems, worries, and heartaches. I realized we all could use some healing; some relief from the sadness; some way to fill our lives with happiness, less worry, better health, and more love. Later that night I sent the email below to my brother Gary and my sister Sherri.

From: Lisa
Date: August 29, 2015 at 11:47:11 PM CDT
To: Sheryl and Gary
Subject: What is the meaning of the tree of life?

This is where it all began...our lives truly are based on the events of Adam and Eve so many years ago. We must free ourselves of the cards handed to us from our ancestors of so long ago.

The Lord has led me the way to do it in all the spiritual guidance the past months.

Today I saw a family in motion and yet so much sadness deep within. Everyone was there, and yet everyone appeared miserable in their lives. The same way Lenny felt. The Lord is giving us a chance to better ours, a chance of freedom; freedom from ourselves, our hidden conscious that plaques our lives. I am on the journey to freedom and happiness and I know it's out there for you too.

It's time to change the way we feel, the way we move, and the way we love. It is amazing how I can already feel a change in myself since finding out about the tree of life, why people don't heal, but how they can. I am sending you an article that will start you on the journey, if you are interested. I am also sending you another email. Go through the imbalances down the chart. Which ones apply to you, your health, or your life? There are seven categories called chakras. Google them to find out more.

A must read book is Why People Don't Heal, But How They Can by Carolyn Myss. We can pray to God, love Him, and worship Him, but until we heal ourselves we will never have the true happiness that was meant for us. You will need this to get your mindset of what is really going on in your life. I'm still reading and learning here and not even sure what I am doing, but I do know I was led here, and I am already feeling better but I haven't even begun.

Love love love you! Goodnight! Prayers for healing! P.S. Gary, hope your ankle is better. Get the book in the library or online, and it will help your pain!

A DAY OF THERAPY

After my latest research I headed outdoors after getting home from church. The sun is the energy source to charge our batteries and today I decided to charge mine. I had read this in the latest book I was reading, so I sat in the backyard on an old-style swing all afternoon.

I closed my eyes and went through the affirmations on chakra healing that I had written down. I had the paper in my pocket along with my stones. It was comforting, swinging, with the sun beating down on my back, and my mind releasing negative energy. Our lives carry many deep wounds, past experiences, and grudges, but often we don't even realize it. After supper I again took a bath and relaxed my mind, removing unwanted past judgments.

PART THREE: CAPTURED FOR THE TRUTH

SEVEN SACRAMENTS

My research on the chakras is very interesting. I found out they are recognized by most religions in today's times, and are symbolized as the Seven Sacraments of Christianity. They represent the energy of life dating back to centuries ago, representing one's religion and faith, daily life, and wellbeing.

Each chakra has a name and place in your body that holds those sacraments. The first is called the Root Chakra located at the base of the spine, representing baptism into Christ; the second is the Spleen, located in the lower abdomen representing First Communion; the Solar Plexus is the third chakra for Confirmation, located at the stomach; and the fourth is the Heart in the center of the chest, the Sacrament of Marriage. The fifth chakra is the Throat, representing the Sacrament of Confession; the sixth is the Sacrament of Ordination on the forehead, and the seventh is the Extreme Unction on the crow of the head. These are the power of life; all emotions, stress, past errors and judgments live upon these, and if they are not open, or functioning correctly, our life, health, and wellbeing are affected.

WEEK ONE

My boss was on vacation so I would be working all week; something I don't normally do. The alarm went off and I rolled over, hit off, and jumped out of bed to get into the shower. This was unusual for me because I am a two snooze person. I arrived at work early and the morning flew by. We kept busy and I was in a great mood. I seemed to have a sense of restored energy.

It was amazing how I felt, so easy, relaxed, and energized. I got home from work, changed clothes and told Al I was going out to charge my battery and sit in the sun. I returned to the swing at the fire pit and enjoyed the beauty of nature; the warmth of the sun on my back; and the music playing on the speaker. My mind felt at ease and I again began saying the affirmations in my head, adding a couple of new ones today.

Tonight I would remove any past errors and judgments I hold on myself, and others. I never imagined I could be holding onto grudges on past events, but maybe I did. I began releasing things that had upset me over the years; people who had hurt me in some way.

Being small can have its advantages and disadvantages. I was born tiny and grew up being skinny. We know some people get nicknames; some by choice, some not so. Mine growing up was "skinny," and not by choice, of course. It bothered me but there was nothing I could do about it. It was kids being kids and part of growing up. So tonight I am going to remove that nickname from my negative experiences.

The next day, like yesterday, I jumped out of bed, showered, and got ready. Again the day was steady and time seemed to be going fast. I received a call from a customer who was somewhat disgruntled with questions and complaints. I seemed to handle the situation fine. Later my co-worker told me she couldn't be nice to everyone; there were some people who rubbed her up the wrong way.

I enjoyed the relaxation of the sun therapy and I decided to do it again today. After I needed to pay bills and work on them while Al made supper. There were papers lying on the desk which needed picking up first; the query and submission letters I had written for my book, folded in thirds. I had it in my purse to show the family one weekend when I was in Salina but never got them out. I later took them out and threw them on the desk.

As I picked up the three fold papers something fell out of them. I pick up the small piece of paper that had fallen on the desk. It appeared to be a copy or a receipt for a First Communion Rosary. It looked old. The back was darkened, and it also had a couple of holes in it like staple holes. Where in the world had this come from and what is it telling me?

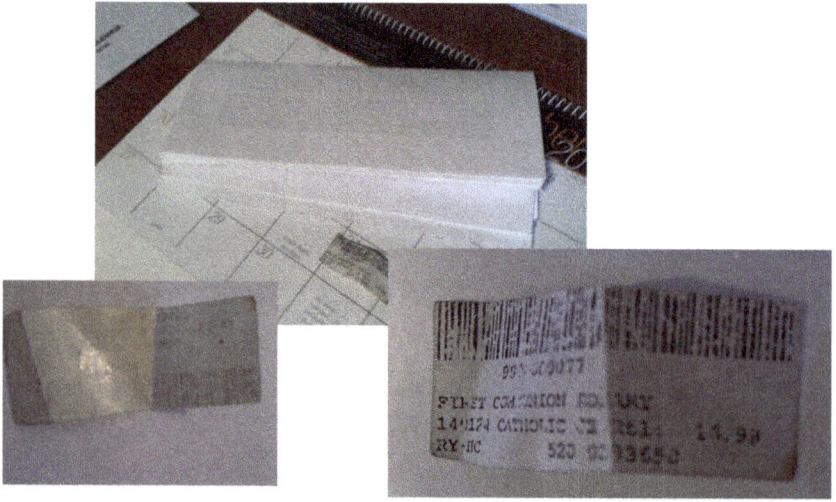

I ran to the Shop Quick to get cigarettes. As I pulled into the garage on my return, and turned the car off, my eyes were drawn to the speedometer. It read 119680. The number 1968 was sticking out. In 1968 I would have been eight years old, which is the age I made my First Communion. I had just found a receipt for a First Communion Rosary, and I'd learned of the connection and healing relationship between the chakras and the Seven Sacraments. Also, Lenny was born in 1968. There has to be something to it!

All in all this week went well. My energy level had definitely increased and I felt much more relaxed. It also seemed the tension in my shoulders was gone, but how could that be? I had never been able to get rid of the shoulder stress.

WEEK TWO

I continued the ritual as well as I could. Our weekends were always booked, so I couldn't work on myself as much as I would have liked. I had also been trying to write my book in between and it was difficult as there did not seem to be enough time.

I liked the motivation I felt, though. I had a new sense of self-esteem. I got in contact with Gary and Sherri to see if they were able to get a copy of the book, or even the stones. I had been sending them emails on the chakras as well, along with websites they might want to check out. I decided to order them both a paperback book, so I knew they would receive it.

On the twelfth day of my alternative therapy I headed towards the swing to sit and relax, enjoying the feel of fall in the air. I closed my eyes, unwinding from the day. My mind repeated my affirmations, I released some more emotions, and I thought about my book. The signs, messages, uncertainty, my sanity, the psychic, and the chakras, they were all happening for a reason; all leading me to a better way of life, health, and happiness.

When I opened my eyes there was a shadow in the yard in front of me, a cross with the electrical poles. I take photos with my phone. My mind tells me, without a doubt, I am on the right track.

I now thought I had an answer to one of my questions – the something needing to happen. I suddenly felt that something was happening. I had a new confidence, a new courage, and a new sense of wellbeing, again leaving me no doubt that everything was happening for a reason.

I realized I needed to let Andrew know and bring him up to speed on what was going on. I called him and we spoke for a long time, as I sat on the swing outback. He was doing well but felt unsure about where life was taking him. As I told him of my newest journey I rattled on so fast I think he wondered what I was on. It was this new self-esteem, driving me, exciting me, and wanting to share. I told him about my next book, the chakras, and the book he needed to read.

DREAMS

On my first visit to the psychic she asked me, "Are you having dreams?"
I answered, "No."
And she came back with, "Well, you are having dreams, but you aren't seeing them. You will in the future." On the second visit she asked how I was sleeping, and if I was having dreams yet. I told her that I was still not having dreams and my sleeping was not good. I was having night sweats, and menopause symptoms. According to the chart I was told I should not be in menopause. The things I was experiencing were all part of this "blockage" I had.

I have tried to have dreams, if that's possible. As I lay in bed that night my mind went into semi-sleep mode, where you are just starting to fall asleep, but not deeply yet. The place where you may see an image, and once you recognize it, you switch your eye motion, and it's gone.

Sherri was having dreams. She sent me an email about them, and they were different every night. She was opening up, learning the truth about her energy of life, and changing her thought processes. She also had a dream right after Lenny died. He was looking at her, not saying anything, but he wore a look of sorrow knowing the pain we would go through.

It was Sunday, we had left church and we were a few blocks away from home. I asked Al, "What does God look like?" He seemed irritated by it. I explained we know what Jesus looks like as we see him on the cross, in church and everywhere; But what about God? Al didn't answer.

Al didn't know I had the vision a few nights ago. I saw someone at the side of the bed; he was dressed in a white robe and was holding a book in his hands, waist high so I could see. His hair was whitish gray and shoulder length, and he had a long beard and mustache. He gestured to sit down to sit and read the book, my book. My eyes flinched, and I looked to see him, but he had gone.

As we were driving home from church, I told Al of the vision. I also told him that Sherri was having dreams, and I told him the reason why I had asked what he thought God looked like, the person I saw.

THE FIGURINE AND THE PEOPLE

When I first discovered the trashcan in the garage with the "figure" in it I obviously didn't know what to think. But the first thing was I wanted to see if everyone else could see it also. It was pretty surreal and crazy, and kind of spooky! As I shared it with family members and friends it became apparent I was not the only one seeing the figure in the trash can, and the faces within, as well as in the other photos. Some people believed it to be spirits of past souls. My search continues to explore the acts of God, the mystery of angels, signs, the spirit world, and eternal life and reincarnation.

WINFIELD FESTIVAL

The Walnut Valley Music Festival is held every year in Winfield Kansas. Same as last year, we made plans to meet Kenny and Cheryl at the park in Winfield. From there we would follow each other into the campsite, which was being saved by their longtime friends, and we would set up camp.

It was not a hot day but after setting up the tent, the bed, and the area, we were sweaty and thirsty. Cheryl and I went into the camper to catch up with the girls. We exchanged stories, laughed, and enjoyed seeing each other again. About thirty minutes later we decided we should probably go out and check on the guys.

It wasn't long until the girls yelled at us to come over and get a temporary tattoo; they were sitting outside the campers and had an assortment of them. I grabbed my drink and headed their way. We were all laughing and searching for my tattoo. I told them I wanted a butterfly, but then again, I see hearts too. Decisions, decisions! I found one of each, I wanted them both. Amy wet the paper towel for application. She told me to put my foot on the cooler so she could apply it. I did. As we sat there, talking and laughing, she said, "I don't remember you being like this."

I laughed and replied, "I wasn't." We all laughed. I told them I was on a new alternative therapy and that I was writing a book about it, but it was deep. They were interested in hearing about it but we all agreed that now was not the time as we were having fun.

At the festival sleep is a rarity as the music goes on all night. So do the crowds. Because of this we stopped off to get ear plugs on the way. They might help to block out the late night noise. After walking the grounds for most of the evening and listening to the bands on Stage 5 we were exhausted. We hit the portable mattress bed at around 1:30 a.m. I slept well, considering the conditions.

Sleeping late was not an option as there was too much going on outside. I got up and felt good, with no aches or pains. By mid-morning we were having bloody marys and screw drivers. We had no place to be until 1:00 p.m. when we would head to the main stage for the band playing then. Clouds were starting to build up around us but it was not clear whether rain would hit. In Kansas you never know.

At 12:30 p.m. we headed up the hill to the main stage inside the fairgrounds for the 1:00 p.m. performance. The announcer came on to announce the band and stated it looked like the rain and weather should miss us. The gentleman sitting in front of us showed us his phone with radar and said he wasn't sure about that. The band played two songs and it started to pour down rain with thunder, and lightening. The grandstands dispersed and people ran back to their camps or to the barns.

We hung out at the campsite all afternoon, during which time the rain became lighter and turned into a light mist. By late evening it had cleared. We walked around the campgrounds as Cheryl was looking for someone she knew. We never did find him but we laughed a lot. We ended back up in the fairgrounds listening to the bands playing on different stages.

PART THREE: CAPTURED FOR THE TRUTH

The temperature had dropped and it was cool and damp from the rain. I hated sleeping this way; the dampness and coolness was not my cup of tea anymore, but we made the best of it. We put our earplugs in and attempted to sleep.

Al, Kenny, and Cheryl went to have a shower at 6:30 a.m. as they wanted to beat the rush and the line. I slept in and climbed out of the tent at around 9:30 a.m. They each experienced different showers, each having their own story, but something they all had in common was that you had to pull on the chain and hold it for the water to come out.

Al walked with me to the shower. The line wasn't bad - there were only ten people in front of me. A man in line a few spots before us was telling the person next to him about the chain pulls; he said you needed to bring in a weight to hang on the chain to keep it running.

When my turn came I got shower number 7. There were two rows of showers; each with about ten showers; making about twenty showers available for $5.00 a shower.

In the shower, I pulled the chain to release water; it was nice and hot and felt good with the open sky above. After washing with one hand I reached for the shampoo and out of habit I took my other hand and poured shampoo in the palm of my hand. I put the shampoo down to wash my hair. I was halfway through shampooing my hair when it dawned on me, the water was running, as both my hands were in my hair. I didn't have anything heavy on the chain holding it down. Did I get lucky or was some force helping me out, holding it down for my convenience? I continued the rest of my shower, cream rinse and all, and when done, I reached up, pulled on the chain, and shut it off. Thank you spirit!

Al, Kenny, and Cheryl were ready to take chairs up to Stage 5; it was going to be a beautiful day and we planned to sit there for the afternoon. Since I was not ready yet I told them to go on, and I would meet them up there when I was done. I went to the camper to use the electricity to dry my hair; the gals were in there. After I was done we sat and talked. They spoke of another friend who hadn't come this year as her son died and it was a bad situation. It was then that I brought up my brother's suicide, the events that had been happening, and my book. I also brought up the butterfly dance and the song playing when I recorded it; "A Simple Man" by Lynard Skynard. I asked if they knew it. Rhonda said her son was getting married in the spring and that was their song to dance to. Goose bumps, again.

We had been sitting at Stage 5 for a few hours, moving closer to the stage as people exited. We ended up center stage only four to five feet away. People were coming to listen to their favorite band and sat in front of us on their blankets. We were having so much fun.

We were close enough that we could walk to camp easily to refresh our beverages. I had just returned and the others were now ready, leaving me sitting by myself. As I set there a group came and sat in front of us, possibly a family; maybe a dad, his daughter, and his grandbaby. It wasn't long before the gentleman pulled a book out of his backpack.

The name of his book caught my eye. He was sitting in a low to the ground camping chair so it was easy for me to look down and see the book in his lap. I saw the name of the chapter, and then another and it sounded so much like what I had been experiencing. I couldn't help but ask him what he was reading. He told me explaining the storyline and said his book club was reading it. I told him the title and the chapter I saw reminded me of a book I just read. I told him the name and he said "this one is fiction." I sat back and watched him turn the page, to the next chapter, and I saw the title: *You Have Been Called*. I was amazed and wondered, could this be yet another message? A message telling me I have been called.

Time goes so fast, especially when you are enjoying yourself, your company, and the surroundings. Sunday was here already, it seemed, and we were loaded up, and ready to depart. We said our goodbyes and ventured towards home. It was amazing how well I felt considering the late nights, the sleeping conditions, the walking of the campgrounds, and the beverages consumed throughout the three days. I didn't ache nor did I feel exhausted. In fact, I felt great. I carried the chakra stones with me all weekend and they appeared to be making a difference in the way I felt. When I got home, instead of hitting my recliner and relaxing like I'd normally do, I washed the laundry, the sheets, the blankets, and our clothes.

PART THREE: CAPTURED FOR THE TRUTH

SO CLOSE TO ME

Have you ever had the feeling of being watched; the feeling that someone is lurking? I have always wondered if my Dad was my guardian angel. Today with media and internet you hear of many events where people were saved by their Guardian Angel.

On my first visit to the psychic I was told there are three very close angels with me. It was asked if I knew who they were and I nodded my head; my Dad and my two brothers. I was told I have spirit guides and they would help me and guide me along the way. When you get a feeling, a sense; something popping in your head, or even a voice, alerting you to something that is about to happen, this is your spirit guide communicating with you. The same guide who alerted me back in March to share my story.

There were a few days back in July when I felt this presence, as if eyes were watching me. At one point I felt a presence over my right shoulder. It was kind of unnerving at first, but over time I began to realize it was my angels watching over me, and I had nothing to worry about.

SMOKED "BUTTS"

Around our house a smoked butt usually means there is pork on the smoker, but tonight we were talking about other smoked butts. I hadn't been out back for a while as fall had arrived and the air was cool. We have a dog run out in the porch for our dog Buddy to go in and out. We also have horseshoe pits way out back and if he went around them the wrong way he may get stuck on the stake. Today was one of those days. As I exited the patio door to retrieve him I noticed cigarettes butts in a drip pan, sitting next to my ashtray, on the table directly out the door. As I continued on to unhook Buddy I wondered why the butts were in the pan, as I certainly hadn't put them there. It had been cool and we hadn't been out back. Nobody had been out there for a few weeks. Returning inside the porch I checked out the butts closer. There were four of them, scattered throughout the pan. It looked like they had been smoked to the butt and then left to go out. I had Al come and take a look and after observing for a while all I could say was, "Looks like the boys needed a smoke." We looked at each other, smiled, and went inside.

SOUL MATES

I married a pretty amazing guy thirty-four years ago and we're still best friends and companions. Has this last year been challenging? Of course it has, as nothing in life is easy. We faced the challenges together. Did Al question things? Yes, he did. How could he not? Things got hairy back in May when the trash can appeared and he told me he thought I was a grieving sister, hurt and lost in my brother's suicide. That hurt like hell.

I know Al believes. He was brought up with as much faith as I was and he has seen everything going on. I know he too believes spirit is near. We joke back and forth about the numbers and time of day; his favorite is "it's that time of day, twice a day." I know that but every time I look, the angel numbers are there. Driving to Aggie Ville to eat one evening we saw the 555 tag on our way down a back street; we laughed. While waiting on Colton to show up he asked the time. I looked at my cell phone lying on the table; it was 5:55 p.m. Again, we laughed.

He knew what was happening and encouraged my treatment, my sun time, my bath time. When I was too busy and missed a few nights, he asked what happened to my therapy. That's why we are still married, as we are support for each other. And now, two months into my therapy, he can see there is a difference in my behavior, my attitude, my self-confidence, and my stress/anxiety. He made fun of my stones at first, saying it was "voodoo," but I know he is only joking.

One night I snuck my bag of stones in the back pocket of his jeans I knew he would be wearing to work the next day. I was home the next day when he came home for lunch. I gave him a hug and searched for the bag in his pocket. I couldn't feel it and he grew suspicious. He went to the restroom and returned with the bag in his hand saying, "Good try." Since then he continues to carry them when he remembers, which is more often than not.

A CALLING

Writing is something I've always enjoyed. As a child I remember writing a diary. Later I wrote poetry; always personal. But never had I thought of writing a book, a story, something to share with the world. If someone would have told me on January 1st of this year that I would write a book, and publish it this year, I would have told them they were crazy.

But here I am, typing away, telling yet another personal story I was given to tell; a story of belief, faith, healing, and the many ways of Our Lord. My Guardian angels, spirits, and spirit guides have guided me to find the truth of life; with that came the healing of my mind, my body, and my Soul.

When I wrote and named *Signs for my Soul* I had no idea that the name would prove to be so true; the signs were truly meant for my Soul, leading me through a journey to find my purpose in life. And now I will be self-publishing a book about my brother's suicide and where it has taken me. My story will heal many hearts and souls. God placed this journey upon me and gave me an opportunity to share my talent and spread His story, providing blessings to me and my family in return. I set the goal to publish the book for my 55th birthday, on November 17th. I believe it is meant to be, and the timing is perfect. The angel numbers have pushed me along, told me to publish, and there's no better time than now.

PROGRESS

Healing takes time. You will never get over losing a loved one, but time can heal some of the wounds. It became apparent that I had been shown the way to spiritual healing. My therapy consisted of sun, affirmations, emotional releasing, baths, incense, stones, music, books, and videos.

There has been great progress since I began this journey. The shoulder stress has gone, my lack of self-confidence has gone, the inability to express myself has gone, the IBS cramping and stomach spasms have gone, the aches and pains of age have gone. Even money stress and anxiety has dramatically reduced. And a rash on my skin which I've had for a long time has almost disappeared.

I have always been a worrier. It is amazing when you learn to calm your mind from the brain fog of everyday life, how it can change your way of life. Positive thinking brings positive results.

Things are changing, I am changing. I now find myself much more at peace with myself and my life. It has taken my nervousness, paranoia, and anxiety away. I am excited about my wellness, my new freedom, and my book.

I have always thought of myself as a confident person; confident in what I do, and the outcome. And yet, I always sat in the back of the room, not daring to go to the front, in front of the crowd. It was safer at the back, out of sight. Now suddenly I was spreading my wings, no longer avoiding the front. Now I am a social butterfly talking to everyone.

Sherri, the first to take the chakra challenge, has blossomed. I haven't personally seen her since she started but I can tell it through her voice, her emails, and in her online pictures and posts. She has a different rhythm and a glow that shows her happiness within.

Gary carries the stones faithfully but is behind with the reading, the affirmations, and the depth of it all. The first book sent to him was the wrong book so he waited another week for the next one. He couldn't get into it and couldn't see how a book would help him to heal. I told him that God and the angels send their messages and healing power through people, books, music, and a myriad of other ways. He will get there. I have faith!

ANGELS

There are many Angels, Archangels, Cherubim, Guardian Angels, and so on. They are beautiful, carefree, winged visions of light showing the mystical work of God. They are told to be beings of light and love, here to teach us lessons, to stand beside us, and lead us in life. The experiences I've encountered have been of a true angelic form.

In death we return to the ground, to dust, and the spirit leaves the body. My belief has always been the spirit of a loved one rises to the skies into the heavenly realm. That spirit may have eternal life according to God's word. We all have our own visions of what an angel is. But I think we can all agree that whether it is the spirit, an angel, or God, it is a blessing from above.

ETERNAL LIFE

How far I have come, from the normal routine of daily living, to the depths of who I am and what I've been given, all driven by the spiritual force that leads me searching for answers to an unknown. As I look back to the beginning, and my original request to God, it was to receive a sign of eternal life for my brother. With this request He has answered me in many ways. I realize I may never know the true meaning of what I will now call a "totem" of souls, but what it, and the other photos can represent, is the many faces, the many lives and souls, of another dimension; another realm, that are indeed in eternal life. And with that I can believe my brother(s) have eternal life with God.

MIRACLES

I have spoken about all of my immediate family in the book but one and I can't leave him out. He is the special one; the miracle one. He is my younger brother Eric and he is handicapped.

Born breach, a leg broken in delivery, and with definite defects of his body, my parents were told he may have days to live. It was said he would never leave the hospital, and if he did, it would be to go to an institution. Hospitalized for the first three months of his life he only left to see a doctor in the neighboring town, his leg in a cast. I remember Christmas caroling at the hospital that Christmas for Girl Scouts. As we walked by the nursery all the girls were looking at the poor little baby lying in the crib, whispering amongst themselves about the things they had heard.

Mom and Dad were told of a doctor in Topeka they should see, as maybe he had recommendations. The doctor in Topeka recommended a non-profit organization to call. He also recommended going to the KU Medical Center in Kansas City. He said Eric needed to be at home, where there was love. He came home that day and his life began.

Over the next five years he had numerous surgeries to his legs, his feet, his arms, and his hands. They were all clubbed as the muscles hadn't grown, and neither had his body parts; they were all curved in. He was in and out of the hospital many times for months at a time, coming home with full length body casts from his waist down to his toes. He had arms casts and hand casts to keep his limbs from curling back in after surgeries. After that came the braces to learn to walk, with a walker.

At home there was therapy after each surgery when the casts came off. We kids helped to stretch his muscles, arms, and legs. As he lay on the floor in front of me one afternoon, when I was 12 or 13, I was stretching the muscles on his leg when we heard a small pop. Lenny ran across the street to get Mom and Dad. Upon x-raying his frail bone we were told it had a slight crack, enough to put him back into another cast. I felt so bad for him, and me. It was an accident but I felt awful, and perhaps still carry the guilt with me.

His growing up days were not easy; he was behind in so many ways, it was hard for him to fit in, hard for him to find a job, and hard to do much at all. He endured the name calling and being made fun of, but he overcame it. Eric is 44 now and he has lived on his own for over twenty years. He plays pool and is well known in the pool arena of Western Kansas. He is a member of the American Pool Players Association (APA) and has been to, and shot in the APA Tournament in Las Vegas three different times. He is on three different pool leagues and he can dominate any table. Anyone coming in who doesn't know him, and wants to play him, doesn't know what they are up against. He is not just a handicapped guy; he is a pool shark, and a champion. God gave him a gift to fulfill his life with.

A NOTE FROM THE AUTHOR

Spirit messages can come to us in many ways. You've now read about all the different ways spirit has come to me. I originally feared telling the whole story, but I realized that without sharing everything, the faces and the trashcan, the story was incomplete. There have been many lessons over the past year which brought me healing of another level. Not only in the death of my brother but for life in general. His words will teach us we are not here for ourselves, but for others. We are a friend, a parent, a sister, a brother, a child, and a teacher; and we are the light and hope to someone else. We must first learn to give, and then we too can receive; we reap what we sow, and we receive what we put out to the Universe. Karma is real and all things happen for a reason. And most importantly, if we can learn to quieten the mind, we will reap the rewards of a better kind.

My journey has brought me healing I never knew I needed, and I know it will help others in return. In prayer we state, "He is the maker of all things visible and invisible and gives us everlasting life." He has shown me this to be true. There are many meanings in my journey. Always have faith, always believe, and always trust your inner self, your guidance, your spirit guides. If you feel it, it is true. Enjoy the present, as it only happens once. Leave the past behind you, forgive, and love like you want to be loved.

The contents of this book are my own interpretations of the readings I have read and researched in the past year. The healing that has worked for me may not work for everyone. There are so many ways to release the negative and find the positive. If we can change our energy we can change our life; if we can change our way of thinking, it can change our outcome in life; and no matter what, always continue to have faith.

Suicide is one of the saddest things one can go through. Not only for those left behind, but for the victim it takes; the battles they fought in life which pulled them down. The emotions displayed in my book are emotions people go through on any given day. True emotions of everyday living, from everyday events, whether it's how you are treated, the sudden death of a loved one, a sudden illness, or life in general; it affects our emotions, our mind, and our Soul. We must learn to leave the negative behind us and forgive, live for the present, and most of all, live for the good of our own wellbeing.

After reading my book it is my hope that more people take the "Chakra Challenge;" a journey to open up their minds to achieve a better mindset, better health, and way of wellbeing. Research the chakra charts and find your weaknesses, illnesses, and health issues, as well as emotional challenges. You will be guided from there. There are also many books and YouTube videos to assist you. Too many people take their life. Did you know that twenty-two soldiers a day take their life? That alone is disheartening. I wish they would have known of the chakra system. When I tell people my story, and about the chakras, no one has heard of a chakra, not even the doctor. It is my belief He is telling us it is time. To find your true purpose and happiness in life, you must learn about, and open your chakras!

We all have dreams and writing and this book have now become one of mine. Another is for there to be a place where those who have lost faith in themselves, and life, can go to help them overcome their fears and rekindle their Divine spark in life. I have designed the "Chakra Challenge" as a fun way for people to learn there is an unknown path. Lastly, I have started a Facebook page called, "Signs for my Soul" where you will find the signs I continue to receive, and also share your own. You will find inspirational quotes, messages of the chakras, spiritual healing, and love! It is our purpose in life to give, to share, and to love; with that I must share. May it help many overcome their obstacles in life, give hope to others their deceased loved ones are in eternal life, and lead to many new beginnings!

A SPECIAL THANK YOU

I want to thank my immediate family for letting me share such personal events in our lives. Our love is for eternity.

A very special thank you to my husband Al, who has traveled the journey with me and has forever loved me. I can't imagine taking this journey without you by my side. You have stayed with me throughout and have been my earthly savior. Without your support and continued love I may not have made it. It brought many challenges to our life, but it has made us stronger. You are my true soul mate.

And most importantly, I must thank God, for He is the true savior. It is His presence in my life that has given me comfort and peace, and made me who I am today. In faith I believe "God is Real," "Heaven is Real"; and whether it is the Holy Spirit or the Holy Ghost, through God, "Spirit is Real" too!

My love to you all!

ACKNOWLEDGMENTS

Ronald McDonald House®

Carrie Underwood: Amazing Grace and
How Great Thou Art

Jill Henwood: Here I Am Lord

Libby L. Allen:
Heaven is My Home Now

Sarah McLachlan:
Will You Remember Me?

Bob Seger – Ride Out Tour
Kansas City, Missouri

Lynyrd Skynyard: A Simple Man

And

Carolyn Myss PH.D copyright ©1977 by Caroline Myss
Why People Don't Heal and How They Can.
Carolyn Myss-1st ed.
R726.5.M98; 1977;
EISBN: 978-0-8041-5085-9

THIS OLE' HOUSE OF OURS
Lisa Leikam, Christmas 1992

This ole' house of ours
Will share another Christmas hour
It's been years of laughter and joy
And oh yes, how many toys?

This ole' house of ours
Has blossomed many beautiful flowers
With pebbles blowing their own way
But always a home to come and stay

This ole' house of ours
The memories go on for hours
Birthdays, slumber parties, and dances too
We were luckier than we knew

This ole' house of ours
Has given us many powers
Love, laughter, and even tears
Bringing us closer through the years

This ole' house of ours
Will share another Christmas hour
Once again we will unite
For a very Merry Christmas night

MERRY CHRISTMAS
2001

So, you say that paybacks are hell
With that remark, I wish you well.
I say getting even is better
So now you have another letter.

Christmas is a time to rejoice
The Holy birth of Jesus Christ
He gives us the faith to give and love
From his power up above

Take a look around and see
What he gives to you and me
Our wonderful home and a great family
With precious gifts under the tree

Big and small, short and tall
It's not the size that counts at all,
The meaning of Christmas is what it's about
Now get ready, let's all shout

Go North, then South
Go East, then West
Or then again
Which one is best?

Is it up
Or is it down?
It's time to search
Just look around

It could be open, it could be closed
Look ahead: you might see your nose
It could be dirty and then be clean
But no, it's not the washer machine

Well now you have it, that's all you get
It's time to find that special gift
We give this to you with all our love
As I said, with help from above

ABOUT THE AUTHOR

Lisa Leikam was born and raised in small town USA, La Crosse, Kansas, and currently resides in Manhattan, KS. This is her first published book. It tells of her personal experiences before and after her brother's suicide, leading her through an indescribable journey.

She started her rewarding career as a dental assistant, which was her profession for twenty years. From there she became a Licensed Insurance Agent in the State of Kansas and did this for three years until she landed a legal assistant position for a reputable attorney and law firm in Salina, Kansas. She worked here for six years where she learned to write, edit, proofread, and compile error free work.

After moving back to Manhattan, Kansas she now works part-time as a Licensed Insurance Representative. She enjoys life with her sons and their friends, her husband, her family, and friends. They are avid Kansas State Fans and have grown up with the KSU family. Writing has been a passion of hers from an early age, writing personal poetry of life events, and memories. She also loves to refurbish or "uplift" things. She believes there is much beauty in the old.

www.ingramcontent.com/pod-product-compliance
Lightning Source LLC
Chambersburg PA
CBHW040554010526
44110CB00054B/2698